How To Tune, Repair and Regulate PIANOS

A Practical Guide

Illustrated

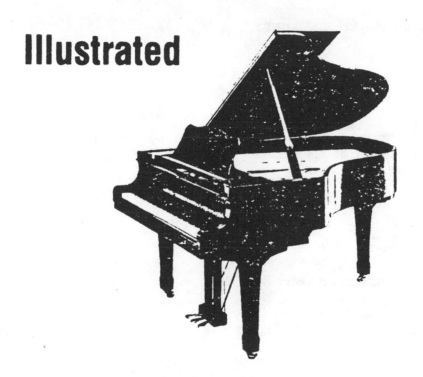

Jack Bradley

Hill Springs Publications

5023 Kentucky Street
South Charleston, West Virginia 25309

First Edition

First Printing

Copyrignt © 1985 by Jack Bradley

Printed in the United States of America

Library of Congress Catalog Number: 85-60253

Bradley, Jack
How To Tune, Repair And Regulate Pianos – A Practical Guide – Illustrated
Includes index

ISBN 0-931856-04-3

Published by
Hill Springs Publications
5023 Kentucky Street
South Charleston, WV 25309
SAN 211-5735

Contents

b # b # b # b # b # b

To Louise and Patti, whose assistance and encouragement were invaluable.

Preface

Welcome to the world of Piano Technology. The object of this book is to instruct in the servicing of acoustic pianos and to enable a person with little or no previous knowledge of the instrument, after the necessary study and practice, to properly tune, repair and regulate pianos.

It is estimated that in the United States alone, there are over 15,000,000 pianos, with an additional 250,000 sold annually. Considering that all of these pianos need servicing and there are only about 5,000 qualified technicians and another 4,000 with varying degrees of qualification, the need for good piano technicians is quite evident.

The piano is an old and honored instrument that has for many years been considered a symbol of artistic taste, accomplishment and even status and a good piano technician is respected and welcomed.

Unlike other books on this subject, this book assumes the reader has little or no previous knowledge of pianos or music and does not have the ability to read music. Alos, the use of highly technical data and math is omitted in these studies and is not considered necessary in the practical applications of the information presented here.

Most of the methods described in this course have been developed and used by professional piano technicians for many years and are taught in technician's schools around the country.

With the proper motivation, anyone can develop the skills to enjoy piano work as a hobby or build a profitable business for part or full-time work. Like most other skills, piano work requires a measure of common sense and is "ten percent talent and ninety percent work." If everything were easy, the pleasure of accomplishment would seldom be experienced.

It is necessary for the student to have access to a piano during the study of this course. If one is not readily available, getting the use of one or acquiring a used piano at very little cost is explained later.

Merely **reading** this book will not make a Master Craftsman Technician. It will, however, show how to develop the skills to service pianos, and, if so desired, become an independent professional business person.

Let's begin.

"Nothing in the world can take the place of persistence. Talent will not. (Nothing is more common than unsuccessful men of talent.) Genius will not. (The world is full of educated derelicts.) Persistence and determination alone are omnipotent."   (Herbert Hoover)

Section 1. The Piano And Its Parts

A BRIEF HISTORY OF THE PIANO

Though the information in this brief history does not apply to the actual servicing of the piano, it would enhance the technician's image if he had knowledgeable answers to questions customers pose. In any case, possessing background knowledge of whatever a person may be working with is heplful.

Ancestors of the modern piano date back to antiquity. Around 2600 B.C., the Chinese used an instrument known as a "Ke". It had color-coded strings and bridges on a wooden box; the colors representing different moods.

The Greeks and Romans, about 100 A.D., languished to the sounds of the single-stringed "Monichord", which had a movable bridge.

The "Clavis" (meaning keys), came into use on church organs after 1000 A.D., which led to the "Clavichord", used in the 16th century. Also in the 16th century, a man in Venice named Spinetti, constructed a larger instrument known as a "Spinet", which was also known in England as the "Virginal".

During the late 16th and early 17th centuries, the "Harpsichord" came into popularity. It was still larger and more powerful than the Spinet and more improvements were made including the addition of pedals, which made it the favorite of musicians of the day who wrote considerable music for it, including Beethoven's Moonlight Sonata, written around 1802.

The piano actually came into being in 1711. Bartolomeo Christofori, of Padua, Italy, invented an instrument he called "Piano-a-forte, with a sturdier case than the harpsichord to withstand the pressure of larger strings, which greatly inproved the tonal quality, and an action (moving parts) with hammers and a much-improved mechanism. This innovative instrument made it possible for a performer to use "expression", and for the first time, to control the touch and volume of the instrument.

From the 1750s, many improvements were made and much effort was devoted to getting away from the wedge-shaped, space-consuming grand piano. In the 1770s, the "square grand" was developed but the tone was not up to the regular grand.

Improvements continued to be made upon the square grand including the iron frame and "over-stringing"; having the bass strings higher and at a cross-angle to the treble strings, thus allowing them to cross each other and reduce the size of the case.

In the early 1800s, the vertical or "upright" piano came upon the scene. By 1860, the trend toward the upright was in full swing – so much so that in 1880, the manufacture of the square grand was discontinued.

The development of the upright was spurred on after the 1880s by the "invention" of apartment houses and the necessity to conserve space.

The era from 1900 to 1930 was the heyday of piano manufacturing with over three hundred companies competing in the United States and Canada.

Economy and space had a hand in design of the smaller pianos of the 1920s and 1930s, such as the studio, console and modern spinet, that could be sold for prices the average person could afford and would fit in the smaller houses and apartments.

By the 1970s and 1980s, the number of manufacturers had dwindled to less than twenty five with conglamorates buying up many of the old names. Also, a goodly share of the U.S. market had been taken over by Far East manufacturers such as Yamaha, Kiawi and Samick.

PIANO TYPES, STYLES AND CASES

The five basic styles of pianos, from the smallest to the largest are: spinet, console, studio, upright and grand. The first four of these are known as "verticals" because of the general direction of the strings. The strings on a grand piano are horizontal.

Pianos are made in a wide variety of wood finishes and in black and white. They are also available in many sizes but the verticals take up about the same floor-space; approximately 57 X 26 inches. A generally accepted rule-of-thumb is: the larger the piano, the better the sound.

Identifying the style is usually a simple matter of the piano's appearance, the exception being that of the spinet and small console where the position of the action (moving parts) is the deciding factor. The spinet has a "drop action"; that is, some of the moving parts are below the the back end of the keys, which 'pull' the mechanism. All the other verticals have a "direct action"; the action is <u>over</u> the ends of the keys and pushes the mechanism.

Here are some approximate piano style sizes:

Spinet   36 to 38 inches high.

Console   39 to 43 inches high.

Studio   44 to 54 inches high.

Upright   48 to 66 inches high.

Grand   5 to 9 & 1/2 feet long.

The size of the grand piano is determined by measuring from the center of the back edge of the lid, to the front edge of the case beyond the keys, parallel to the hinged side of the lid.

b # b # b # b # b # b

The Five Basic Styles Of Pianos

Spinet

Console

Studio

Grand

Uprignt (Player)

VERTICALS

The term "vertical" refers to the position of the plate and strings of the piano and includes the spinet, console, studio and upright – in fact, all pianos except the grand. This vertical family comprises the majority of pianos in use and will be the one you will be servicing the most.

As you can see in the diagrams further on in this section, the mechanism of the vertical is different from the grand, but the basic principle is the same; Finger power is carried from the key, through the capstan or sticker, to the wippen, to the jack, the hammer butt, the hammer shank, the hammer, to the string. The resulting vibration of the string and the path of sound processing is explained in the section "The Piano's Sound".

THE PIANO TECHNICIAN

In contrast to the name "piano tuner", a piano technician not only tunes, but is capable of handling almost any problem that may arise concerning acoustic pianos. To put it another way, a piano technician is a piano doctor.

A piano is a precision instrument with over ten thousand parts, made from materials from all over the world, and it should be treated with respect. A quality piano is designed and constructed with enough sensitivity to enable an accomplished player to convey the emotions of the music; from his brain, through his fingers and the instrument, to the ear of the listener. This is carried to its fullest potential with the concert pianist, who is required to portray over fifty emotions via his fingers and a well-tuned and regulated concert grand piano.

Anyone wishing to be proficient in piano work should develop skills in the use of hand tools. They are extensions of the hands and a source of income.

A piano technician should always apply his skills to the best of his ability, remembering that every customer is entitled to a piano in the best possible condition under existing circumstances.

ACQUIRING A PRACTICE PIANO

As you will be repairing and tuning the piano as practice, you do not have to be as particular as a person seeking a piano in good condition for playing purposes – therefore, the price you pay for one can be much less.

There are still many old upright pianos in homes and churches, most just collecting dust in a corner. Many owners will gladly part with the old "relic" for $25. to $50., and some will let you have the piano for nothing, just for taking it off their hands. Remember though, when you're moving a piano you will need some help, preferably experienced help – and when a large upright and/or stairways or narrow doorways are involved, be sure to take measurements. In some cases involving these situations, it might be better to either continue your search or consult a professional piano mover, the names of which any piano dealer could supply you with.

Look for pianos for sale in the want-ad section of the newspaper or Shopper's Guide. Ask your friends and the local music stores to be on the lookout for a cheap one for you. If all else fails, run an ad in the "wanted" section of the newspaper classifieds, but you really shouldn't have much trouble getting one for your studies.

Another way to gain the use of a piano is to ask a music store or a friend or relative who may have an old piano, if you can use it to practice on and fix it up for them in the process, as payment for its use.

Before you negotiate any deal however, make sure the piano is structurally sound and that it does not have a split pinblock or bridges. These problems can usually be detected by loudly striking several keys, up and down the keyboard. It doesn't matter if the piano is badly out of tune, you can take care of that later. What you will be listening for is any harsh "rattles" or strange "gurgling" sounds when the keys are struck. These kinds of noises indicate a structural problem. Also, if several of the strings in one area are extremely out of tune, in relation to the rest of the piano, this usually indicates a split pinblock. These are the two main things to avoid.

It isn't important if a few hammers are broken off or even a few strings missing; these you can replace. But stay away from the piano that is really junk. After all, you want a piano that is repairable – one that you can sell after you have fixed it up – and for much more than you paid for it.

If you are fortunate enough to run across a bargain in a smaller piano, so much the better. They are easier to move and will bring a higher price when restored.

Still another way to acquire a piano is to rent one from a music store. This is alright for tuning practice, if you're careful, but it doesn't allow the freedom to experiment and repair that you would have with a piano of your own.

GETTING STARTED

One of the first things for an aspiring piano technician to do is acquire a parts and tools catalog from one or more of the large piano supply companies. (See "Useful Lists" in Section 6.) They usually sell only to the trade, (piano technicians, music stores, etc.) but if you write them and explain that you are studying to become a piano technician, they will cooperate. Most catalogs cost a few dollars but they are well worth it and are indispensable.

It is also a good idea to have some inexpensive letterheads printed with your company name (example: Smith Piano Service), address and phone number.

These can be used later for ordering parts and tools, correspondence, and customer billing. They make a professional impression. After you have a few letterheads printed, you can run off more copies on any good copy machine.

THE PIANO'S SOUND

The unique sound of the acoustic piano is produced when felt hammers strike the steel strings, which are stretched to prescribed tensions over the cast-iron plate. This causes the strings to vibrate and produce a sound which is transmitted through the maple bridges to the spruce soundboard, which, in turn, amplifies the vibrations into the sound heard by the ear.

Varying degrees of quality in design, materials and workmanship, along with the size of the soundboard and the lengths of the strings, create the almost individual tonal quality of a piano.

OPENING THE PIANO

Most pianos are quite simple to open. Some require a little searching – and a few appear to be designed by a Chinese puzzle maker.

It makes a better impression on the customer if you go right into your work without a lot of searching and fumbling. A little experience, and imagination in some cases, will take care of that.

When servicing verticals, the first thing in your tool kit to reach for is the "lid prop". (See tool pictures.) This little item serves the dual purpose of holding up the lid and at the same time putting it in the correct position to throw the sound in the direction of the tuner.

Next is removing the front or "music desk". This is the front of the piano, between the lid and the fallboard. Some fronts have slotted brackets, some have catches with flip levers and some have screws that must be removed. In some spinets and consoles, after the levers have been flipped and/or screws taken out, slide the unit forward toward the keys to remove.

Some Everett and Sohmer studio pianos require a 3/16 inch Allen wrench to remove three screws in back that hold the lid hinges. When these are out, slide the lid toward the back and lift off.

Probably the easiest of all the brands of pianos to get into is the Yamaha, which was obviously designed with the piano technician in mind. No tools are required to open the piano for tuning, to gain access to the pedals and trapwork, or to even remove the action.

On grands, most music desks slide off toward the keyboard. The ones that do not have either small screws at the sides near the back or slots somewhere in the slide rails. These can be found by pulling upward on the music rack while sliding it back and forth. When the slot is found, that side will come up and the unit can be lifted off.

It is a good idea to carry a set of piano lock keys in your kit. These are available at piano supply houses and are very inexpensive. About four different keys will open nearly all pianos. This simple precaution could save you much anguish later; especially in churches and schools, where "who has the key?" is a frequent situation.

b # b # b # b # b # b

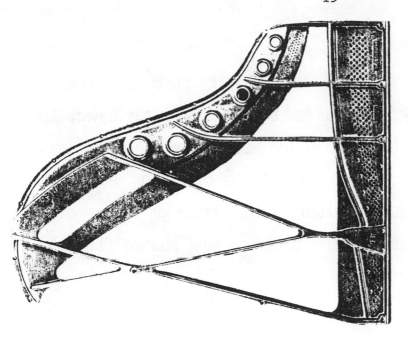

Top left: Plate for a grand piano.

Top right: Tuning pins in laminated pin block.

Below: Plate with soundboard, bridges, strings and tuning pins driven into the pinblock (not shown) before it is put into a studio case.

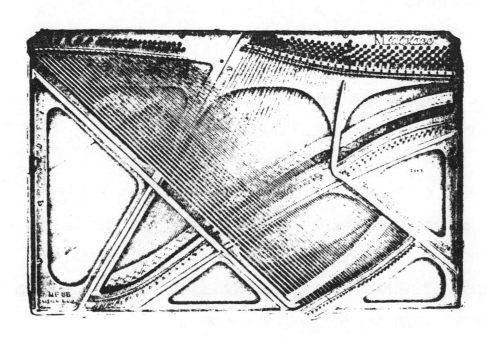

THE PLATE

The plate could be considered the skeleton of the piano. It is made of gray cast iron to which carbon graphite has been added and has a very low level of thermal expansion. At the top of the plate are holes for the tuning pins and at the bottom are hitch pins for fastening the bottom end of the strings. The plate material is well suited for its purpose of supporting the twenty tons of pressure exerted by the tension of the strings. Plates are finished in gold bronze.

THE BRIDGES

Spaces are designed in the plate for the curved rock-maple bridges that are glued to the soundboard. There is usually a separate bridge for each of the three sections; bass, tenor, and treble. These bridges are fitted with "bridge pins" that hold the strings in place that pass over them.

THE SOUNDBOARD

The soundboard is the amplifier of the strings and is actually the speaking voice of the piano. It is usually made of thin spruce and is slightly convex toward the strings with a "crown" in the center. Its shape is maintained by "ribs", which are fitted and glued diagonally to its back.

THE PIN BLOCK

In a way, the pin block is the "heart" of the piano and has very much to do with how well a piano stays in tune.   It is made from 5 to 45 cross-grained laminations of maple and other hard woods, glued together to form a "plank" which runs the width of the piano.

The pin block is fastened behind the top of the plate and the tuning pins are driven in at a 5-degree angle,(leaning away from the strings). The friction of the tuning pins against the wood resists the pull of the taut strings.

Good pin blocks have a "feel" and the tuner can actually feel the pin move in the pin block during the tuning process.

Sometimes pin blocks in older pianos become dry, causing the tuning pins to be loose. This lessens the stability and durability of a tuning job and shortens the useful life of the piano. There will be more on this later.

TUNING PINS

The finely-threaded steel tuning pins are driven into precisely drilled holes in the pinblock for the purpose of holding the strings and allowing them to be tuned.

The end of the string is inserted in the hole provided, 5/8 from the end – then a close, inside coil is made by turning the pin clockwise. The outside end of the pin is square, to fit the tuning lever.

There are about 225 tuning pins in the average piano. They are available from the supply houses in several lengths and diameters; blued and nickel plated.

THE STRINGS

The piano has the distinction of being both a string and a percussion instrument. When the felt hammers strike the strings, the strings generate tones. They could be called the piano's vocal chords. Piano wire is made of fine-tempered steel – the blue-chip product of the steel industry.

As the scale of the piano descends, the diameter of the wires increase;

from a #12 or #13 size wire at the top of the treble, to as much as a #24 at the bottom of the tenor section.

The core of the bass strings is also steel but is copper wound to add mass, thus creating a lower tone. The upper bass uses two or three strings for each note and as the tones get lower, these graduate to larger sizes until the last ten or twelve notes in the bass are wound <u>single</u> strings, still graduating to larger sizes.

The strings in the treble and most of the tenor sections are usually three to a note. These groupings of 2 or 3 strings (throughout the piano) are called "unisons". This grouping adds volume and depth of tone.

The unwound treble and tenor strings are attached to the tuning pin, go down over the bridge, around the hitch pin at the bottom, back across the bridge, and up to another tuning pin where the other end is fastened. The "3rd" string in the unison is attached the same way, only when it comes back up, it is fastened to the first tuning pin in the <u>next</u> unison and is tuned to a higher pitch. This procedure is continued on through the last (highest) treble string. The only problem with this arrangement is – if any one wire breaks, two strings are out of service.

The wound strings are all attached to the hitch pins by loops made at the bottom of the string. Here, when one breaks, only one is out of service.

THE KEYBED

The keybed is made up of three wooden strips known as: the front rail, the balance rail, and the back rail. These are held together by four connecting cross-pieces. This framework supports the keys which are held in place by steel pins fixed in the front and balance rails. Felt-lined slots in the keys fit over these guide pins, allowing the keys to rock freely back and forth.

To insure quietness and proper touch, the back rail is covered with a wide felt strip, while the balance and front rails have felt washers that fit over the steel pins and under the keys to cushion them. The felt washers and strip beneath the keys are known as "underfelts".

THE KEYS

Piano keys are made of light wood, usually white pine or spruce. Except for the very old and the very expensive new pianos where ivory is used, keys are topped with plastic. The black keys, commonly called "sharps", are made of ebony-wood or plastic.

The standard piano keyboard is made up of 52 white keys and 36 sharps, making a total of 88 keys, or 7 and 1/3 octaves. The keyboard is laid out in a pattern so each octave of 12 keys is identical in appearance.

The keys rock back and forth over the balance rail of the keybed and should all move freely and uniformly.

Functionally, the keyboard is divided into three sections. From left to right, the Bass section, (about 28 keys, from A-0 to C-3). In the center, the Tenor section, (about 30 keys, from C#-3 to F#-5). And on the right side, the Treble section, (about 30 keys, from G-5 to C-8). See Master Chart.

MIDDLE C

"Middle C" is the main reference point on a piano keyboard. Its location is the white key, just to the left of the two black keys near the center of the of the keyboard, opposite the name or trademark of the piano.

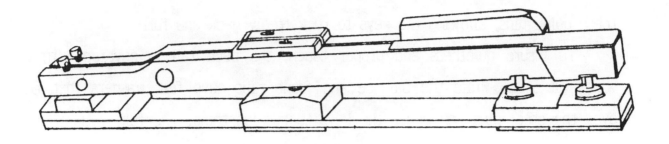

Above: Cross section of keybed showing one white key and one sharp in place.

Below: Bottom portions of bass and treble string sections showing difference in hitch-pin attachment.

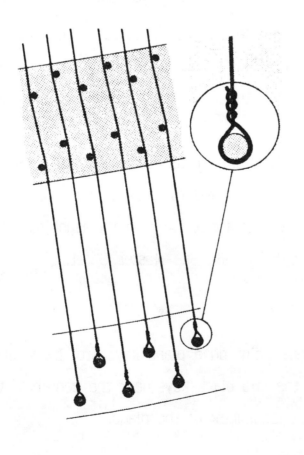

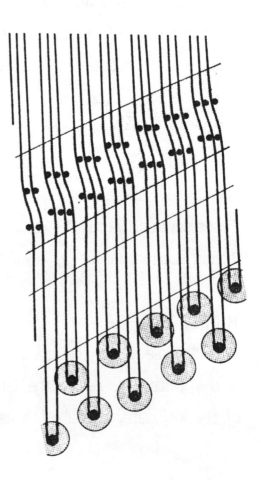

Master Chart

WHITES			SHARPS		
CPS	Key#	Location#	Key#	Location#	CPS
27.500	1	A-0	2	A#-0	29.135
30.868	3	B-0			
32.703	4	C-1	5	C#-1	34.648
36.708	6	D-1	7	D#-1	38.891
41.203	8	E-1			
43.654	9	F-1	10	F#-1	46.249
48.999	11	G-1	12	G#-1	51.913
55.000	13	A-1	14	A#-1	58.270
61.735	15	B-1			
65.406	16	C-2	17	C#-2	69.296
73.416	18	D-2	19	D#-2	77.782
82.407	20	E-2			
87.307	21	F-2	22	F#-2	92.499
97.999	23	G-2	24	G#-2	103.83
110.00	25	A-2	26	A#-2	116.54
123.47	27	B-2			
130.81	28	C-3	29	C#-3	138.59
146.83	30	D-3	31	D#-3	155.56
164.81	32	E-3			
174.61	33	F-3	34	F#-3	185.00
196.00	35	G-3	36	G#-3	207.65
220.00	37	A-3	38	A#-3	233.08
246.94	39	B-3			
261.63	40	C-4	41	C#-4	277.18
293.67	42	D-4	43	D#-4	311.13
329.63	44	E-4			
349.23	45	F-4	46	F#-4	369.99
392.00	47	G-4	48	G#-4	415.31
440.00	49	A-4	50	A#-4	466.16
493.88	51	B-4			
523.25	52	C-5	53	C#-5	554.37
587.33	54	D-5	55	D#-5	622.25
659.26	56	E-5			
698.46	57	F-5	58	F#-5	740.00
783.99	59	G-5	60	G#-5	830.61
880.00	61	A-5	62	A#-5	932.33
987.77	63	B-5			
1046.5	64	C-6	65	C#-6	1108.7
1174.7	66	D-6	67	D#-6	1244.5
1318.5	68	E-6			
1396.9	69	F-6	70	F#-6	1480.0
1568.0	71	G-6	72	G#-6	1661.2
1760.0	73	A-6	74	A#-6	1864.7
1975.5	75	B-6			
2093.0	76	C-7	77	C#-7	2217.5
2349.3	78	D-7	79	D#-7	2489.0
2637.0	80	E-7			
2793.8	81	F-7	82	F#-7	2960.0
3136.0	83	G-7	84	G#-7	3322.4
3520.0	85	A-7	86	A#-7	3729.3
3951.1	87	B-7			
4186.0	88	C-8			

Bass

Middle C

Treble

The Action

The large assembly containing most of the moving parts of the piano is called the "action". It is removable as a unit to facilitate repairs or to take into the shop for more extensive refurbishing.

Most actions have standard, interchangeable parts, many of which can be used in pianos of different models and manufactures. This greatly facilitates the work of the technician and makes it possible to repair most pianos in the home without carrying a large supply of parts.

There are three common types of actions; the "direct action", in the console, studio and upright — the "drop action" in the spinet, and the grand action.

REMOVING THE VERTICAL ACTION

The actions of these verticals, console, studio and upright, are the easiest to remove. Simply unscrew the action bracket bolt knobs and lift out the action, being careful not to damage the damper felts on the bracket bolts as you lift it out. Sometimes it is also necessary to remove one or more of the pedal rods — but this is a simple matter. Most vertical actions have "feet" so the unit can stand upright on a hard, flat surface.

REMOVING THE SPINET ACTION

The spinet action is a little more complicated to remove in that the sticker-wire button assemblies must first be detached from the keys. While holding the back end of the key down, pull up on the sticker assembly, then slip it through the slot in the back end of the key.

Next, remove the key stop rail and remove the keys from the keybed, making sure to <u>keep them in order</u>. As a precaution, use the edge of the key stop rail to draw a straight line from the back end of key 1 to just behind the key top of key 88. Should the keys accidentally become mixed up, this line will serve as a quick guide for returning them to their correct order. If a suitable flat surface for storing the keys in order is not available, remove the bottom board from the piano and place it between two chairs to make a "table".

Remove the screws from the bottom of the action brackets. Use a length of twine or small flexible wire to contain the sticker wires so they will not fall and be damaged during the action removal and replacement process. This is done by tying the string or wire around one of the end brackets, then run it along the outside of the stickers, looping it through the middle brackets. Pull it snug and tie the other end to the opposite end bracket. Remove the pedal rods and the action is ready to lift out. Again, be careful with the damper felts.

This seems like a lot of bother but sometimes it is the only way to gain "exposure" to a problem or a defective part. With a little practice, spinet actions can be removed in just a few minutes. Always attempt to diagonse the trouble before removing the action. Its removal may not be necessary.

REMOVING THE GRAND ACTION

Unlike the spinet and the other verticals, the grand keybed and keys are attached to the action assembly.

Remove the fallboard, key blocks and key slip by taking out their screws. Remove any guide brackets that may be at both sides of the keybed. The action may now be pulled out, drawer fashion, for repair or to take to the shop. Make certain all the hammers are in rest position when pulling out the action and keep your fingers away from the keys. Hammers in the "up" position are easily broken off when pulling a grand action.

The Spinet Piano

- Pin Block
- Tuning Pins
- Keys
- Bridge
- Strings
- Action Assembly
- Hitch Pin
- Soundboard
- Plate

The Vertical Piano

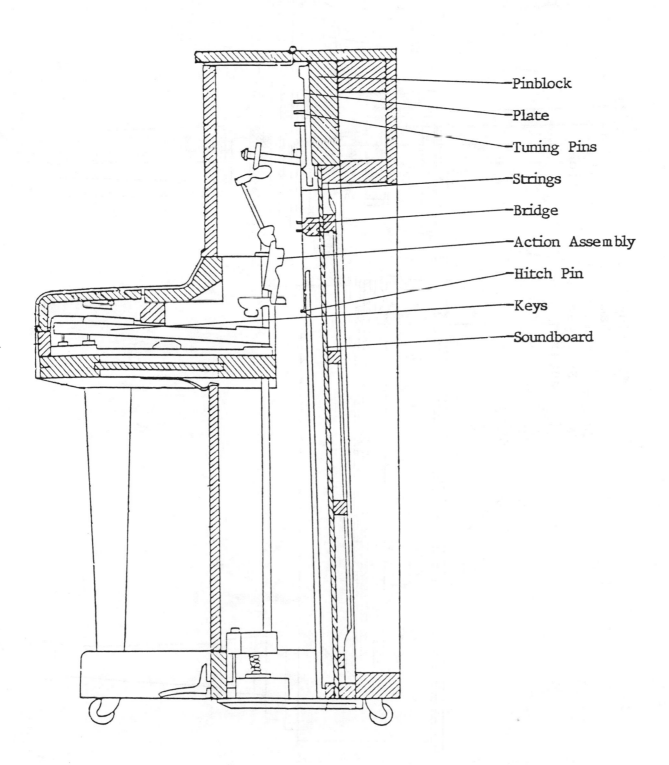

- Pinblock
- Plate
- Tuning Pins
- Strings
- Bridge
- Action Assembly
- Hitch Pin
- Keys
- Soundboard

The Grand Piano

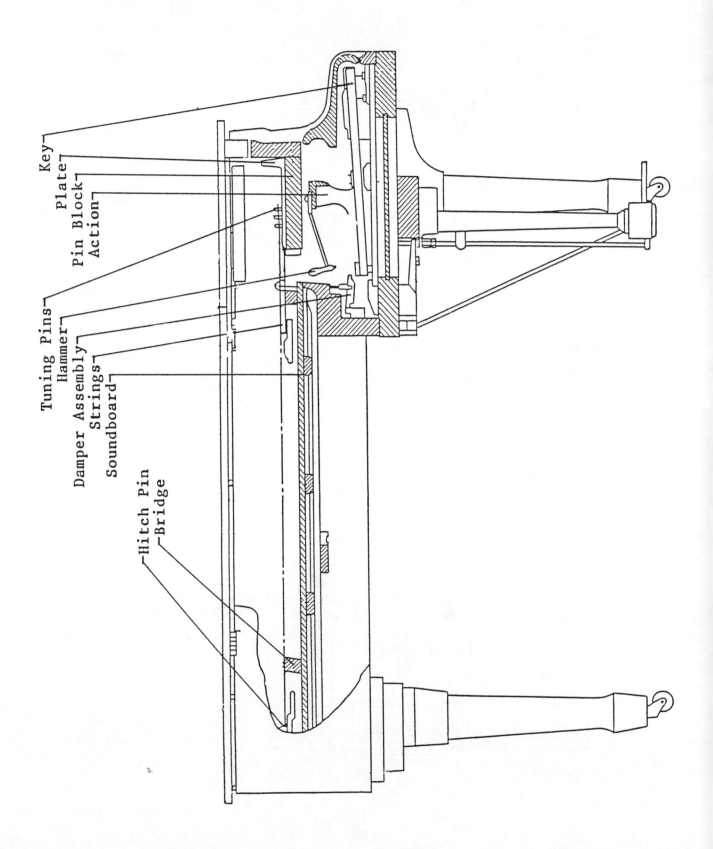

Key

Plate

Pin Block

Action

Tuning Pins

Hammer

Damper Assembly

Strings

Soundboard

Hitch Pin

Bridge

Small Parts

FLANGES

The piano flange is a small part that, together with the center pin, is a hinge-like device that attaches one of the moving parts of the action to one of the action frame rails or to another moving part.

Flanges are made of sculptured hardwood with felt bushings glued in around the holes for the center pins. These pins support the wippen, hammer butt, jack, damper lever and sticker. Except for the jack flange which is glued in, a flange and its attached moving part can be removed from the action for repair or replacement by simply removing an action screw.

There are several sizes and types of flanges and a few of each should be carried in a well-stocked kit, for it is usually more expedient to replace a worn or broken flange than to repair it.

CENTER PINS

Sometimes referred to as "centers", the importance of center pins and their felt bushings cannot be exaggerated. These small, brass-plated steel pins are the axis of all moving parts within the action. They are located in the flanges on wippens, hammer butts, jacks, damper levers, stickers and grand hammer shanks.

Center pins are of many graduated sizes and must fit into their felt bushings with precisely the correct tightness. If they are too tight, the action unit will be sluggish, causing so-called "sticking keys". If too loose, the part will wobble and malfunction.

HAMMERS

The piano *hammer* is the part that strikes the string and has much to do with the tone quality produced by the instrument.

Hammers are made of strips of several layers of shaped and compressed felt, glued under great pressure to a graduated wooden core. When the glue has set, the individual *hammers* are sliced from this strip to a uniform thickness. Since bass *hammers* are shorter (to compensate for the bass overstringing), they are made separately from treble and tenor *hammers*. After slicing, holes are drilled for the *hammer* shanks. Treble and tenor holes are usually drilled straight, while bass *hammers* are drilled at an angle.

Grand *hammers* have curved tails so they may be caught by the backchecks.

New *hammer* sets and replacement *hammers*, which are available in various lengths and weights, should be "voiced" so their striking surface will produce a tone quality to match that of their surrounding *hammers*.

HAMMER SHANKS

Hammer shanks are straight, round wooden sticks made of maple or cedar wood. The standard diameter for uprights and most verticals is 7/32" with a smaller diameter available for some spinets. Shanks are quite inexpensive and are usually purchased by the hundred. It is necessary to cut off a new shank to the required length.

Grand *hammer* shanks are tapered and usually come as an assembly, with the flange, knuckle and drop–screw attached.

b # b # b # b # b # b

HAMMER BUTTS

The maple wood hammer butt serves many functions. It holds the bottom end of the hammer shank and the hammer butt flange that holds the hammer assembly to the action rail, plus the butt felt and the curved buckskin-covered surface that is pushed by the jack, causing the hammer to strike the string. In the upper front of the hammer butt is a short shank, on which is mounted the "catcher". In the back of the butt is a slot to receive the hammer spring.

There are several types and sizes of hammer butts: The most common is the wood flange type. Many foreign made pianos use a butt with the hammer spring built into the butt and flange. Some old uprights use a brass rail butt that attaches with various types of metal plates to receptacles on a brass action rail strip. Then there is the Billings flange, which is a spring-like clip that fits around the butt center pin and slips over the action rail screw.

Grands do not have hammer butts as such. The knuckle on the underside of the grand hammer shank serves this purpose.

JACKS

The wooden jack in the piano performs a function similar to a human arm throwing an object. It propels it; then, at the proper moment, releases it, letting momentum carry the object forward.

In the verticals, the jack pushes the hammer butt; in the grand, it pushes the hammer shank knuckle. When the hammer is almost at the string, the "letoff button" causes the jack to kick out, allowing momentum to carry the hammer forward and strike the string. The jack spring then re-positions the jack in its original position, ready to repeat the operation.

Unless the jack, jack spring and letoff are regulated and working properly, they can cause serious problems for the player.

BRIDLE STRAPS

The purpose of the bridle strap is to assist the hammer in returning to its original starting position.

Bridle straps are made of small strips of fabric with a cork or clip on one end for attaching to the hammer butt catcher, and a plastic or suede tip with a small hole on the other end, to slip over the bridle wire.

SPRINGS

There are several different springs in each piano action unit to assist moving parts to return to their original starting position. The hammer spring and damper lever spring in verticals, and the repetition spring in grands are curved wire springs, while the jack spring in verticals is a small coil spring. There are also the larger springs used in the pedal/trapwork and to shift the grand action.

CAPSTANS

Capstans are usually screws in the top of and near the back end of the keys, and on which the wippens rest. They can be regulated up or down for the purpose of removing any "lost motion" from the action movement.

SPOONS

Spoons are small metal levers at the back of the vertical wippen for the purpose of lifting the damper levers. They are also used in grand wippen and damper assemblies.

WIPPEN ASSEMBLY

The wippen assembly is that part of the action between the capstan and hammer, (containing the jack, etc.) that carries the motion from the key to the hammer.

There are various types for verticals but all operate basically the same.

The grand wippen assembly is completely different from the verticals and can be regulated to a more precise operation.

STICKERS

Stickers are levers which rest on the capstan with the other end connected to the wippen. (Sort of an extension of the capstan.) They are found mostly in uprights and studios — and in spinets, where they connect the end of the key downward to the wippen. Grands and consoles do not use them.

BACKCHECKS

The backcheck is the part of the action that catches or checks the movement of the hammer on its rebound. In the verticals, it is connected to the end of the wippen; in the grand, it is attached to the back of the key.

DAMPERS

Without dampers, intelligent piano music would be impossible because the sounds of the string vibrations would run together and create nothing but cacophony.

The mechanisms of the piano are such that the dampers are normally in a damping position. When a key is depressed, the damper lifts, allowing the string to vibrate freely. When the key is released, the damper goes back in place on the string, quietly stopping the string movement and the sound.

The sustaining pedal mechanism allows the lifting or partial lifting of all the dampers simultaneously, so the player can achieve a sustained (legato), or blending effect of the sounds and string vibrations.

On verticals, damper levers are activated by "spoons" on the back of the wippens. On grands, the entire damper lifter mechanism and dampers are separate from the action unit and remain in the piano when the action is removed. These damper levers are activated by the movement of the back end of the key.

Damper felts are made of wool and are available in many styles, shapes and sizes.

FELTS

Felt keeps a piano from being a noisy, clattering mess. It is used at every point where a moving part makes contact with another moving part.

Felts are used under the keys on all three rails – in the hammers – for the dampers – on the damper levers and damper lifter rods – in all flange bushings and other bushings – in the wippens – on the hammer butts and hammer rail – the backchecks – and in the trapwork.

Piano felt is available in assorted thicknesses and densities and in various colors – in sheets, strips and ready-cut pieces for specific uses.

In time felts wear, compress, dry out, rot, and sometimes are eaten by moths, mice and other creatures. When these things happen the felts must be replaced, the most common replacements being the key underfelts, dampers and hammers.

b # b # b # b # b # b

PEDALS AND TRAPWORK

The three pedals on the piano allow the player to add different "controls" to the music he is playing.

Pressing the pedal on the right causes all the dampers to lift from the strings, allowing their sound to linger or "sustain", hence its name; the sustaining pedal.

The middle pedal has different functions on different pianos. Usually, on verticals, it activates a device to lower a strip of felt between the hammers and strings, reducing the volume of sound. This is often called the "soft" pedal.

On the grand, the center pedal is called the "sostenuto". It allows a bass or tenor note or notes to be sustained, while other notes are played unsustained or staccato.

Pressing the left pedal on verticals usually moves up the hammer rail, which shortens the hammer stroke. To a degree, this decreases the volume of sound and lightens the touch

On grands, this left pedal causes the action to shift slightly in the case, moving all the hammers so they strike only two strings of the three string unisons, and only one string of the two string unisons. This is the grand's soft pedal.

Trapwork is the term used for the brackets, levers, rods and springs, etc. that connect the pedals to the action and dampers.

On the grand, the pedals and rods are held in a pedestal-type frame called the "lyre", while the trapwork is suspended above it under the keybed.

....

Vertical Action Assembly

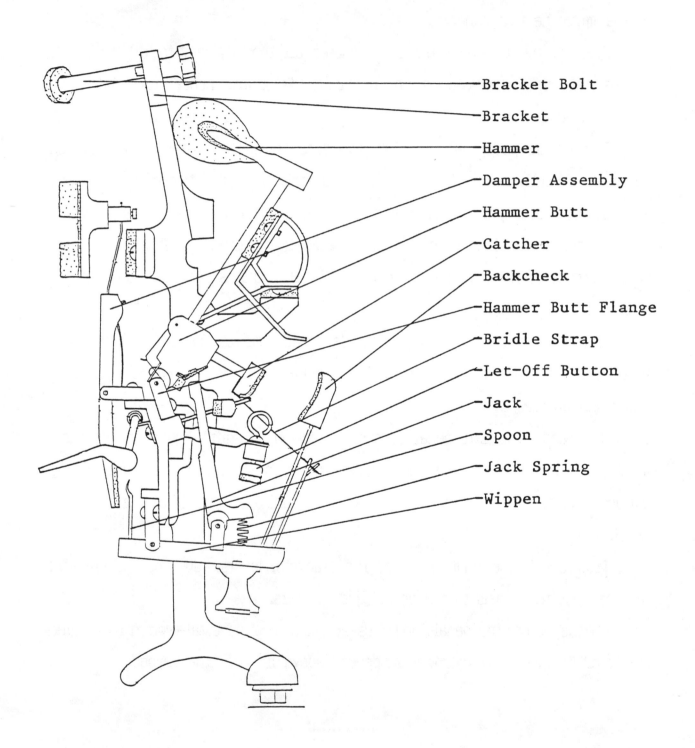

Bracket Bolt

Bracket

Hammer

Damper Assembly

Hammer Butt

Catcher

Backcheck

Hammer Butt Flange

Bridle Strap

Let-Off Button

Jack

Spoon

Jack Spring

Wippen

Vertical Wippen Assembly

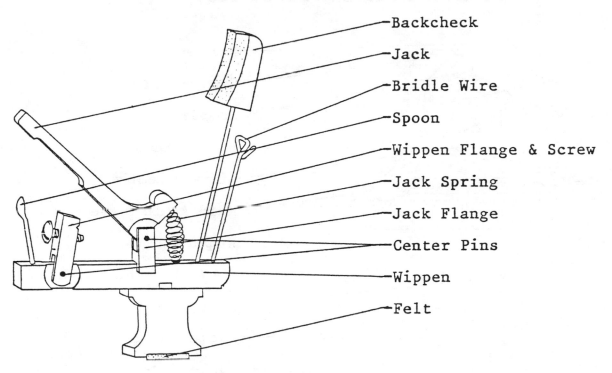

- Backcheck
- Jack
- Bridle Wire
- Spoon
- Wippen Flange & Screw
- Jack Spring
- Jack Flange
- Center Pins
- Wippen
- Felt

Vertical Damper Assembly

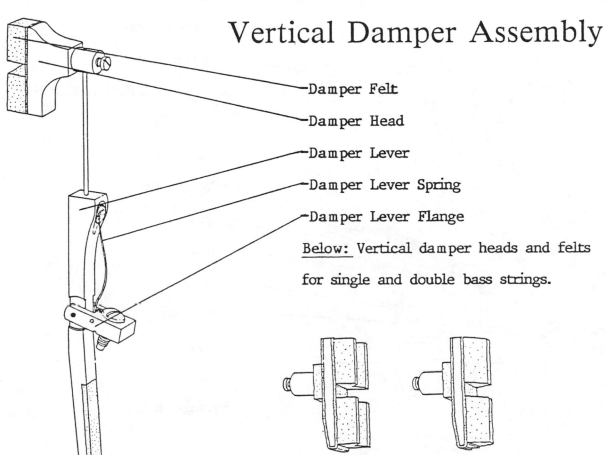

- Damper Felt
- Damper Head
- Damper Lever
- Damper Lever Spring
- Damper Lever Flange

<u>Below</u>: Vertical damper heads and felts for single and double bass strings.

Grand Action Assembly

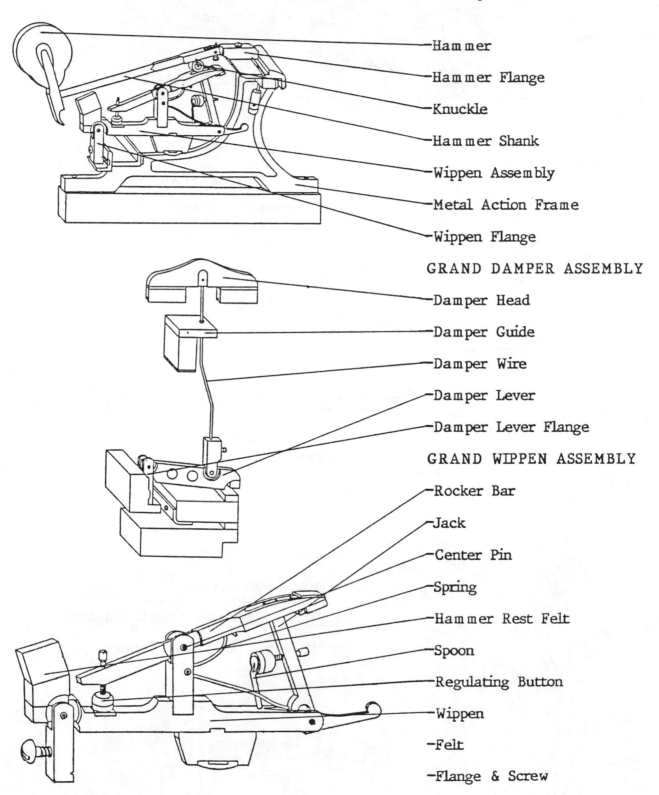

Hammer

Hammer Flange

Knuckle

Hammer Shank

Wippen Assembly

Metal Action Frame

Wippen Flange

GRAND DAMPER ASSEMBLY

Damper Head

Damper Guide

Damper Wire

Damper Lever

Damper Lever Flange

GRAND WIPPEN ASSEMBLY

Rocker Bar

Jack

Center Pin

Spring

Hammer Rest Felt

Spoon

Regulating Button

Wippen

Felt

Flange & Screw

Section 2. Repair
Tools

STANDARD TOOLS
Top: L to R.
Technician's Screwdriver
Small Screwdriver
Small Phillips Screwdriver
High-Torque Screwdriver
Locking Pliers
Slip-Joint Pliers
Chain-Nose w/Cutter Pliers
Bottom: L to R.
Metal-Cutting Saw
Adjustable Wrench
File

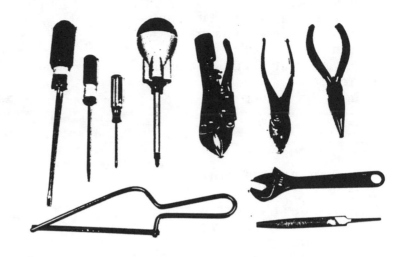

MISCELANEOUS TOOLS
Top: L to R.
2 Piano Lid Props
4 Piano Lock Keys
Small Scissors
Screw Holder-Inserter
Small Flashlight
Magnet
Jack Spring Hole Reamer
Bridle Strap Inserter
Butt Plate Inserter
Bottom: L to R.
Dust Brush
3/16" Allen Wrench
Flange Spacer

KEY TOOLS
L to R.
Key Easing Pliers
Brad Inserter
Key Dip Block

REPINNING TOOLS
Top: L to R.
Chain-Nose Pliers
Diagonal Cutters
Tuning Pin & Center Pin Gage
Center Pin Hole Reamer
Center Pin Punch
Hammer & Combination Handle
Bottom:
Center Pin Holder

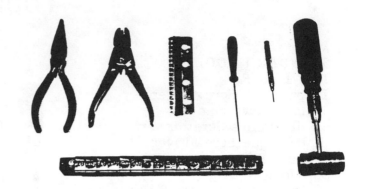

HAMMER REPAIR TOOLS
L to R.
Hammer Head & Butt Extractor
Hammer Shank Clamps
Voicing Tool
Grand Shank Press
Hammer Shank Cutters
Combination Handle
Hammer Shank Reducer
Hammer Shank Drill Bit
Bottom:
Sandpaper File

RESTRINGING TOOLS
Top: L to R.
Technician's Screwdriver
Hammer in Combination Handle
String Inserter
Tuning Pin Setter
T Handle
Tuning Pin Punch
String Lifter & Spacer
Locking Pliers
Chain-Nose Pliers w/Cutter
Bass String & Tuning Pin Gage
Below:
String Stretcher
Piano Wire Gage
Soundboard Steel

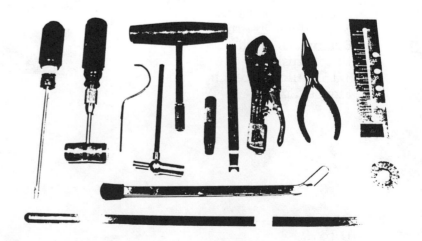

REMOVING THE KEYS

Sometimes it is necessary to remove the keys in order to clean the keybed, replace the underfelts, take in the keys for re-topping, or to remove a spinet action. When you take out the keys, by all means keep them in order or you will waste a lot of time sorting them.

Open the piano as explained in Section 1. Prop up the lid and take off the front and music desk. Next, take off the fallboard and/or key stop rail by removing the screws at each end. Sometimes there are one or two small nuts to remove on top of the key stop rail. This is the wood piece with the felt strip attached that runs the length of the keyboard, behind the sharps. You will notice that in nearly all pianos the keys are numbered. These numbers are stamped in the key wood and are found close behind the end of the keytop or sharp. They run from left to right and are consecutive from 1 through 88.

After the keys have been completely exposed, they can be removed one at a time by pulling the key straight up at the front until the sides can be grasped at the key button. This is the raised wooden piece in the center of the key containing the balance rail bushing. Sometimes in older pianos it is necessary to use both hands to get the key off the balance rail pin because of corrosion on the key pins. If the action hasn't been removed, be careful of the wippens or stickers at the back of the keys.

When the key is off, or nearly off the center key pin, carefully lift the wippen or sticker with one hand while removing the key with the other. This last procedure is repeated in reverse when replacing the keys.

While all the keys are out, it is a good idea to clean the keybed. Most customers have hose vacuum cleaners which are ideal for this purpose. Use the small round brush and the narrow slant-ended attachment and be careful not to suck up any of the underfelts.

GRANDS

Removing the keys from a grand piano is a little more complicated. First, remove the case parts surrounding the keyboard, then remove the fallboard, plus any action guides that may be at each end of the keybed.

Next, carefully pull out the action and place it on a table or between two chairs. Putting it on the floor makes it difficult to pick up.

Take off the key stop rail, then remove the screws you will find at the end of each leg of the metal brackets that hold the action unit on the keybed. These will number from 8 to 12, depending on the piano. Now the action can be lifted off the keybed. Remove the keys by pulling straight up, off the key pins. Keep them in order.

TROUBLE SHOOTING

The first thing to do when inspecting a piano is to play all the keys, one at a time, the entire length of the keyboard. Try to make mental notes of whether a problem is with the key, the action, regulation, the strings, loose tuning pins, dampers, or whatever. An experienced technician can just about determine in this manner what is causing the problems, even before taking the front off the piano.

Next, open the piano, take the front, etc. off and check out the trouble by closer inspection. Take note of any missing strings or hammers, etc. and determine if you have the proper replacements.

If the problem is with the mechanism rather than the strings or soundboard, always begin your diagonsis with the key and work up through the action. Occasionally you will find the key itself is cracked or broken at the center pin hole, so make sure the key is intact before proceeding. Next, with the fingers of one hand, push up the wippen or sticker and hold it while moving the key up and down with the other hand. This will help determine if the key is working freely or if the key bushings are too tight.

Now go through the action unit, following the course of the key motion and checking for problems. Keep in mind that trouble in the unit may be caused by a combination of several problems, especially in old pianos. With practice, you will be able to diagnose piano problems in just a few seconds.

While you are determining what exactly has to be done to get the piano in good shape, check out the pedals and trapwork.

When you have covered the situation, make a mental estimate of how long the job (including tuning) will take. With experience, it is possible to calculate this within ten or fifteen minutes.

About this time, formulate an approximate charge for the customer, allowing a little extra for the unexpected. Also, its a good idea to show the problems to the customer, explaining to them why and what needs to be done and make sure they understand there will be extra charges for repair. On rare occasions, a customer will have the fanciful idea that any repair work goes with the price of the tuning. It would be prudent to have any possible misunderstandings averted before beginning the work.

Check the hammers and dampers for side-wobble, indicating a loose or broken flange, or center-pin problem.

A common situation in old uprights is action foul-ups caused by the jacks working out of their slots, due to the deterioration of the old glue that holds the jack in the wippen. After removing the action, unhook the bridle strap and take out the wippen flange screw. Carefully take out the wippen and the jack and re-glue the jack, making certain it is back in its slot snug and straight. Let the glue set a few minutes before replacing the wippen unit.

Imagination is a big help in solving problems and it is possible to learn something new on almost every job. Don't fear the unexpected. A little challenge makes the work more interesting.

EASING KEYS

Probably the most common mechanical problem occurring in pianos is so-called "sticking keys". The most frequent cause of this is the swelling of the felt key bushings and sometimes the key wood, caused by humidity change. This will cover about 75% of sticking key problems.

Remove the necessary case parts, including the fallboard and key stop rail.

Hold down the sustaining pedal with your foot while softly playing each key along the keyboard three or four times in succession. Holding down this pedal prevents the damper springs from aiding the key return, thus making any border-line sticking keys more obvious.

As you discover the tight and sluggish keys, mark them on the wood part, past the keytop and key numbers, if any.

Next, remove the keys, as described in that section, but take out only one key at a time, work on it and replace it.

While a key is out, inspect the keybed under it for any objects such as coins, etc. that may have fallen between the keys and causing them to bind.

Now take your Key Easing Pliers, which is one of the most frequently used special tools you will have, and carefully place the small side of the nose in the front key bushing slot and gently but firmly squeeze. A little practice will tell you how much but you don't want to over compress the wood and felt (which you can hear when squeezing) as this will make the key have too much side-play and may become noisy and be noticeable on the keyboard. Do the same with the other side of the front bushing. Now repeat this operation with the balance rail key bushing slot. Gently squeeze both sides. This slot will be a little smaller and you will only be able to insert a small portion of the pliers' nose, so do not force them.

Lift up the wippen or sticker again as you did before and put the key back in place in the keyboard. Try it out to make sure the problem has been corrected.

EASING CENTERS

Though not occurring as frequently, what happens to the felt key bushings can happen to the felt bushings around center pins, in flanges on hammers, wippens and other parts. Usually this situation can be alleviated by squirting the affected bushings with "Center Pin Lubricant". available from the piano supply houses.

This fluid is applied from a plastic bottle with a long tube spout to reach into the confined areas of the action. The volatile naphtha carries the residue of oil to the tight bushings, then the naphtha quickly evaporates, taking with it humidity moisture from the bushing and leaving the slight oil residue. Immediately after center pin lubricant is applied, move the affected part back and forth in order to work the fluid into the bushing.

This treatment will correct most tight centers but if the bushing does not respond, it will be necessary to take more drastic measures. Remove the part and apply the lubricant directly to the bushings and work the part back and forth. If the bushing is still too tight, tap the pin out with the center pin punch and measure it with the center pin gauge. Select another pin from your kit, the same size, and insert it and cut it off flush. This should solve the problem. If the center is still too tight, remove this pin and put in the next smaller size. You will see the reason for this procedure after you do it a few times.

OTHER KEY PROBLEM

KEY BUTTONS

The key button is a raised wooden piece near the center of the key containing the felt-lined slot for the balance rail pin. Directly underneath this slot is the hole for the pin. The purpose of the key button is to guide the key, both up and down and left and right. Key buttons are made of soft wood and are purchased in strips of 10 or 12, already bushed and ready to be sliced off with your repair knife as you need them. They are used in both verticals and grands.

REPAIRING AND REPLACING KEY BUTTONS

Sometimes the key button will be split, but all the parts are there and the broken part can be glued back to the remainder of the key button remaining on the key. If part or all of the button is missing or too damaged or worn, remove the key and stand it on its back end on a firm surface, then with your repair knife placed at the point where the remainder of the key button joins the key, firmly push down, separating the button from the key.

Next, with a pencil or pen, make a mark on the side of the key near the top, defining the center of the slot, so you will know where to center the new key button. Slice off a new button, allowing for enough wood to hang over the sides of the key. Take notice of which way the grain of the wood is running when you slice. It makes trimming easier.

Now apply a thin film of glue to both the top of the key and the underside of the button, along the surfaces where they will join. Don't use too much or you will be gluing glue instead of wooden parts. White resin glue such as Elmer's is OK but the so-called "carpenters" yellow resin glues are better as they are thicker and set up faster.

Position the key and button together, taking note whether the long part of the button goes forward or backward. The direction is opposite on whites and sharps. Use the mark you made to center the slot in the button, also center it from side to side, using the adjacent keys to copy any angle involved.

Place the key upright on a flat surface and using a brad inserter, (a small tool for pushing in very small nails and brads, appearing much like a screwdriver – available at tool departments and hardware stores) push a 1/2 inch wire brad into each end of the button, centering between the sides of the key and at the center of the button-wood on each side of the slot. With your repair knife, trim the overhanging wood from the button so it is even with the sides of the key.

Replace the key in the piano in its proper place and with the adjacent keys also in place, try it to make sure there is no binding.

BROKEN KEYS

It is unusual to find an actual broken key but sometimes it does happen, especially with the smaller and inexpensive pianos. This break will undoubtedly be at the center pin hole and will involve a missing or broken key button.

If the key is cracked but still together, try not to separate the parts but bend the key open a little and force some yellow glue into the cracks, using a small stiff-bristled brush or your repair knife. Use just enough glue to make a good bond and be careful not to clog the hole for the key pin.

Check the angle of the glued key to make sure it is the same as its adjacent keys so it won't bind when re-installed. If the key button is missing, replace it, using procedures explained in that section. After you carefully try it for clearance, set this key aside to dry while you are doing other work.

KEY RATTLES

A rattling key is caused by the key bushings either wearing out or coming out. The solution is to replace the bushings. To re-bush a whole set of keys is a shop job but the same procedure applies to 1 or 88 keys.

Remove the key from the piano and with the tip of your repair knife or the blade of a very small screwdriver, remove any residue of the old bushing from the front key pin slot. Cut two small lengths of key bushing cloth, (This can be purchased in rolls) and apply some yellow glue. Also, with the tip of your knife or screwdriver, apply a small amount of glue to the sidewalls of the front slot. Now, carefully position the pieces on the sides of the slot and insert a key bushing wedge. This is a small wooden device for holding the felt bushings in place till the glue sets. When the glue is set, remove the wedge and trim any outhanging felt with your knife. It may be necessary to squeeze the new bushings with the key-easing pliers to insure a free key movement.

If the rattle is caused by the balance rail bushing, simply replace the key button with a new one, as described earlier.

REPLACING INDIVIDUAL KEY TOPS

Key tops are available in different sizes and shades of white and simulated ivory. With old pianos, where this section would most apply, key tops are in two sections; the "front" and the "tail".

Usually only the front needs replacing, however it is wise to carry an assortment of key top sizes and shades, including a few tails.

If there is part of the broken front still on the key and a gentle prying with the knife will not dislodge it, remove the key from the keyboard, stand it on its back end on a firm surface and wedge the knife between the key and old key top and exert downward pressure. This should do the job.

The glue used for repair work cannot be used for attaching key tops as it would make them curl. Piano key cement is cheaply available from the piano supply houses and is a clear "airplane glue" type adhesive. For the kit, a tube of DuPont's Household Cement will do fine.

After you have prepared the key and selected the appropriate key top, apply a thin layer of the cement to the entire surface of both the key and the underside of the key top. Let dry a few seconds and then slide firmly in place. Replace the key in the piano and make a final alignment check. While the key top is drying, be careful not to move it out of alignment when tuning, etc.

REPLACING FLANGES

As described in Part 1, the flanges and center pins are the pivot points of the action. Also, the section on Easing Centers described the treatment of tight flange bushings. However, if a flange becomes broken, the pin works out of the bushing, or the tight center does not respond to treatment, the flange must be replaced.

A word about screwdrivers. In piano work, the screwdriver used most is what is called a piano action or technician's screwdriver. This usually has a 3/16-inch diameter blade, about 6 or 8 inches in length. The tip fits slotted screws and is straight with no flare so it can be turned in places with little clearance.

The procedure described here applies to all flanges on all types of pianos.

The hammer flange assembly on verticals, except the spinet, can be removed without taking the action out of the piano. To do this, first remove the key and unhook the bridle strap. Reach the blade of the screwdriver up under the hammer butt and find the screw head and slowly turn the blade until it finds the screw head slot. Much action work of this type is done by "feel", since it is often difficult or impossible to see all the screw heads inside the action, With a little practice, the ability to "see" with the screwdriver tip can be developed and the work will go faster than when actually looking into the action.

Turn the screw counter-clockwise to loosen, then use the screw holder/inserter to finish removing the screw so it won't fall into the action. Now the hammer assembly can be removed.

To work on flanges in other areas, the action must first be removed. When removing wippen screws in verticals, be careful of your screwdriver blade against the damper lifter spoons.

When you have the faulty flange out of the action, find one in your kit that matches the size of the flange to be replaced. If the old flange cannot be removed without damaging the attached part, lay the flange on its side on a piece of soft wood, (not the piano, bench, or furniture) and with the center pin punch and a small hammer, tap the flat end of the center pin until it protrudes enough from the other side of the flange to be grasped and removed by pliers.

Most new flanges come with long center pins already in them. If this pin is too small for a tight fit in the part the new flange will be attached to, try a larger size from the Center Pin Holder until one is found that will fit tightly. Now try it in the flnage bushings. If it is too tight, enlarge the bushings with the bushing reamer, a little at a time, until the pin fits firmly but not loosely.

Insert the pointed tip of the pin in one side of the flange, center it over the hole in the part and carefully tap it in with a small hammer until it begins to protrude on the other side of the flange. Test with your fingers and make sure the flange moves freely without wobble and is not too tight, or you will be replacing one problem with another. Cut the pin off even with the flange, using side or end cutters and re-install the part.

VERTICAL SPRING PROBLEMS
DAMPER LEVER SPRINGS

The base coil of the damper lever spring is built in the damper lever flange, with the arched arm of the spring extending to the top of the wood of the damper lever where the curved end rides in a slot. If this spring or flange breaks, the damper will no longer seat and cut off the sound. If the flange itself is not broken, replacing this spring with a Damper Repair Spring works quite well and is more expedient than replacing the entire damper spring/flange assembly.

With the technician's screwdriver, reach straight down behind the damper lever and loosen the damper lever flange screw a few turns. Hold the replacement spring in the pliers by the straight end so the opening in the hook on the other end is facing to the right. From the back of the action, facing the damper felts, reach the curved end of the spring held in the pliers through the opening between the damper levers to the left of the damper to be repaired. Position the curved end under the raised screw head with one hand and pull it tight, while the other hand is tightening down the screw head with the screwdriver from above. With a spring hook or the notched end of a bridle strap inserter, push and position the end of the spring into its slot in the upper end of the wooden damper lever.

Cracked damper flanges usually cause side wobble and prevent the damper felt from seating properly. If the flange is cracked, replace it with a new one, which contains a damper spring already built in. Springed damper flanges are available in three strengths: light, for the treble — medium for the tenor — and heavy for the bass dampers.

REPLACING HAMMER SPRINGS

Occasionally you will find misplaced or broken hammer springs on verticals. To reposition hammer springs, carefully reach your open hand behind the hammers, the palm toward the strings and feel along the hammer springs to find if any are out of place. When one is found that is, press the spring with the forefinger and move it over in front of the slot on the back of the hammer butt and release it in place.

To replace a broken hammer spring it is not necessary to remove any parts, though removing the hammer assembly provides a better view.

With the awl inserted in the Combination Tool Handle, reach in between the hammers and make a hole in the spring rail, about 3/8 inch from the bottom and near the stub of the broken hammer spring. Place the head of one of the small screws that come with the repair hammer springs in the screw inserter. Place the screw tip through the hole in the brass end of the repair spring and hold the spring wire tight along side of the screw holder/inserter with one hand, while inserting the screw with the screw inserter into the prepared hole with the other. Give the inserter a few turns while pressing it in until the screw threads have firmly taken hold.

Carefully expand the jaws and remove the screw inserter and finish tightening the screw with a small screwdriver, positioning the spring straight. Now, with your finger as before, reach behind the hammer and position the spring in the slot at the back of the hammer butt. Job completed.

REPLACING JACK SPRINGS

Remove the action and the wippen. With the long-nosed pliers, grasp the remainder of the broken jack spring and pull it completely out. With the Jack

Spring Hole Reamer, ream out the hole, getting rid of the old glue. Sometimes the tip of a knife is also helpful here,

Put a little of the yellow wood glue in the cleaned-out hole and position the large end of the new jack spring down in the hole and glue. Position the other end of the spring in the recess on the bottom of the jack and hold the jack back near the bridle wire. Place a small rubber band over the jack and bridle wire until the glue sets a few minutes.

Choose the correct size, as jack springs come in two sizes: small for spinets and large for other verticals.

GRAND SPRING PROBLEMS

Broken springs on grands are unusual but replacement wippen springs are available at the supply houses. The adjustment of grand springs will be taken up in the section on regulation.

In most grands, the ends of the springs in the wippen assembly are held in place by loops of silk cord. On old grands, these cords rot and break and must be replaced. There are usually two to a wippen, each of which forms a loop in which the end of the spring is hooked and held taut. These loops are anchored in a small hole with a wooden peg.

To replace these cords, the old peg and cord must be drilled out and a new cord and peg inserted. The cord is available at supply houses though other cord or heavy thread may be used, provided it is strong, durable and flexible and of suitable diameter.

With a small drill bit in a hand vise (if you are doing only one or two units) or an electric hobby tool/drill, drill out the old pegs and cords. Make a loop of the correct length and insert in the hole to the proper distance. Now put a little yellow glue on a round toothpick and insert over the cord, wedging it in. With side or end cutters, cut off the excess toothpick and cord. Reposition the spring ends and replace the wippen assembly in the action.

INSTALLING BRIDLE STRAPS

Bridle straps are available with either cork or clip ends and are used only on verticals. The majority of pianos accept the cork straps, which come in short, medium and long lengths and small, medium and large corks.

First, remove the remnants of the old strap by taking out the old cork. This may be done by reaching your finger or a small object behind the old cork and pushing it toward you to dislodge it. Unhook the tip from the bridle wire by pulling it up and out over the pointed end. If the wire is badly corroded, pliers are a help but be careful not to break off the old wire. If the loop in the wire is too snug, insert the tip of a small screwdriver between the loops and pry them apart a little. This will help with removing the old strap and installing the new one.

Cork straps are installed using a Bridle Strap Inserter, which is nothing more than a hammer shank with a very small nail imbedded in one end. Simply push the pointed end of the inserter in the flat side of the cork at one end of the bridle strap. Position it so the strap is on the down side and push it in the hole below the butt catcher, located at the end of the catcher shank attached to the front side of the hammer butt. When the strap is firmly in place, take the vinyl or suede end in your fingers, straighten it out so the coated tip is facing up. Now, turn the tip facing left and slide it up through coil of the bridle wire attached to the wippen. Near the center of the coated end of the strap is a small hole. Force this down over the upward pointing end of the bridle wire and pull it level. Job completed.

Spring clip straps are used when there is no hole for them below the butt catcher. Simply press the clip over the catcher shank and hook up the other end like the cork straps.

It would be wise to carry a set of the medium cork straps and also a few of the clip type.

REPLACING HAMMERS AND SHANKS
VERTICALS

Nearly all hammer and shank replacements will be in older pianos. If the hammer is broken off, look to see if it has fallen down in the action, then remove the bottom board and look in the bottom of the piano around the trapwork for the old hammer. If you find it, check the broken shank on both the hammer and the hammer butt to see if it is broken at an angle and is otherwise intact. If this is the case, put some yellow glue along the break and a little on the round part of the shank near the break. Slip on a hammer shank repair sleeve over the broken shank attached to the hammer butt. This is a section of brass tubing made to fit snugly over the hammer shank. (There is a smaller size for spinets.) Center the sleeve over the break and put in the other broken part attached to the hammer, making sure the hammer is facing in the right direction. Push the parts together tightly and check to see if the hammer is in line with the others.

If the hammer is missing or the shank too badly damaged for repair with a sleeve, remove the hammer butt and if there is enough shank left to work with, use the hammer head and butt extractor, together with a hammer shank clamp to remove the remaining shank parts. Or – simply cut off the old shank even with the butt and hammer and drill new holes,using the appropriate size drill bit in the combination handle. Be careful to get the hole the same angle as that of the old shank, both in the butt and the hammer. Don't drill the hammer hole all the way through.

Put some yellow glue in the hole in the hammer butt and slip in the shank. Reinstall the butt back in the piano and check to see if the shank is straight, compared to the other shanks. Now, with shank cutters or side cutters, cut off the top of the shank, even with the top of the ajoining hammers and put on the old hammer you drilled out — or a new one of the appropriate size and length. If the top of the shank is too big, reduce the diameter a little with the hammer shank reducer in the combination handle. If the shank is still too long, cut it off a little at a time until the repaired hammer is installed even with the adjoining hammers. Put a little yellow glue in the hammer hole and reposition it back on the shank and check for alignment with the other hammers. Also make sure it will strike all the strings it is supposed to. While it is drying, occasionally check for any slipping out of alignment.

GRANDS

As mentioned earlier, the grand hammer shank is not like the vertical and it is best to replace the old hammer shank with a new one with the stem cut off to size. Replacements are available at the supply houses and there is an adjustable shank and flange assembly available that will fit many grands. Sometimes, in emergencies, sleeves can be used but this is not advisable as thay tend to allow the hammer to turn in the sleeve when the glue dries out.

If this is the only alternative, and the shank is broken near the hammer with not enough room to use a sleeve, cut off some of the shank at an angle and reduce it in diameter to fit the sleeve with the shank reducer. Cut a standard vertical shank at an angle and glue and fit it snugly into the sleeve.

Shanks in grand hammers must be removed with a tool called a grand shank press. this is a clamp-like device that fits over the toe of the hammer, then a turnscrew is tightened, pushing the shank from the hammer. Grand hammers are more narrow and fragile than vertical hammers, and attempting to drill out an old shank could be risky.

After the trial hammer fittings, as with the vertical, cut off the shank by degrees until the proper length is reached. Glue the grand hammer on the end of the shank and align, making sure there is no shank protruding, as this will interfere with the grand backchecks. Let the glue dry and the job is completed.

REPLACING HAMMER SETS

Hammer sets are available from the supply houses but it is necessary to give them information about hammer length, weight and bore for the shanks.

It is possible to replace the hammers on the action in the shop, without the rest of the piano, but there is a slight alignment risk involved. Using a hammer head and butt extractor, remove <u>every other hammer.</u> This is <u>important.</u> This way you can use the old shanks already in place, provided they are in good condition. You will also be using the remaining hammers as alignment guides.

Lay out the new set of hammers in order on a flat surface and move every other one out of line a few inches, yet still keeping these also in order.

Clean off the ends of the old shanks with the adjustable shank reducer but do not reduce their diameter. Put a little yellow glue in the hammer holes and install in order and align, using the old hammers as guides. Check the alignment during drying and do not attempt to install the remainder of the new hammers until the first half has firmly set. Again, check alignment.

After the action with the new hammers has been reinstalled in the piano, the new hammers should be voiced. This is explained in the section on regulation.

REPLACING DAMPER FELTS

Dampers sometimes come off and must be replaced. Also, the damper felt may get too compressed or dry and will no longer cut off the sound properly. These too must be replaced.

Damper felts come in sets for vertical treble and tenor dampers, (different for verticals and grands) and bass damper wedges for verticals, ready to install. The bass wedges for grands are usually purchased by the strip for one, two or three string damping, and are cut off to the proper length.

VERTICALS

Individual damper felts are easily installed in verticals by loosening the damper head screw with a small screwdriver and lifting the damper head straight up and off the damper wire. Take off the old felt with the repair knife and replace the damper head back in the piano and reposition it as before. Now select the proper damper felt and put some yellow glue on its red side where it will contact the wooden head block. Slide it between the damper head and the string and position in place. The spring tension of the damper lever against the string will act as a clamp till the glue sets.

INSTALLING VERTICAL DAMPER FELT SETS

This is best done in the shop. After you have cleaned the action with a brush or vacuum, proceed in a similar manner as with the hammer set installation, removing every other damper felt.

This kind of work is best accomplished with the action clamped in an action cradle, where it can be tilted to whatever angle is best for the work.

Tilt the action or lay it on its back so the old dampers are facing up. Using a plastic center pin lube dispenser or oil can filled with household ammonia, moisten the base of each old damper felt with the ammonia, going up and down the line of dampers several times until the old felts are saturated. Allow about 30 minutes before beginning to remove the (every other) dampers. The ammonia will dissolve the old glue and make removing the old felts much easier.

Line up the new damper felts in the proper sequence and notice that the treble felts are graduated in size. Move out every other felt so you have two rows. Now install the felts from row one and align and let dry, using the adjacent felts as guides. Repeat this procedure with the second row of felts. In the bass, make sure the bass wedges change from one to two-string dampers in the same place as the old ones. Also try to keep the angle of the new dampers the same as the old.

Some damper wire regulation may be necessary when the action is reinstalled but this is to be expected.

INSTALLING GRAND DAMPER FELT SETS

Grand damper felts can also be replaced in the shop but getting them out of the piano is a little more complicated.

Remove the grand action and set it aside. Behind where the action was is a row of damper lifters and it is wise to take the height measurement of these lifters before removing the dampers. This will save muuch time later. Beforehand, take a piece of 3/4-inch thick soft wood, approximately 2 inches by 4 inches and drill holes in one side near each corner. Screw in four round head screws that may be turned in or out for adjustment. Capstan screws or tapping screws the same length as the capstans will work fine. Using this device as a gauge, turn the screws in or out until the platform of this legged gauge fits snugly under the grand damper lifter levers. You now have a means of resetting the levers when you reinstall the damper wires and heads with the new felts installed.

You will need still another gimmick before removing the grand dampers. Get a piece of 3/4-inch wood about 5 feet long and 3 or 4 inches wide. Along the center of this board, drill 1/4-inch holes in a row, 1/2 inch apart, the entire length of the board. You will need about 70 holes.

Now, with a small screwdriver, loosen the damper lifter screws and carefully pull out the damper wires and heads and put each as it is removed, in the board with the holes. Make sure to keep them in order. When you have all the damper wires stuck through the board, run a length of masking tape over the damper heads to prevent them from falling out.

Take these to the shop and replace the damper felts. Inspect each damper carefully before removing the felt, to see which type or combination of felt is required for replacement. It is best to remove and replace the grand damper felts on each individual damper before going to the next.

Replace the dampers in the piano and tighten the lifter screws, with your fingers at first, until you align the felts with the strings. Use the damper gauge block you made to find the proper height for the lifter levers. When you have all the dampers aligned properly and they cut off the sound as they should, run a strip of masking tape over the damper heads to hold them steady while you tighten the lifter screws.

INSTALLING STRINGS

Though uncommon, compared to other problems, piano strings do break, mostly on old pianos with rusty or corroded strings, but occasionally on new pianos, due to a flawed string or faulty installation at the factory.

After you know how, installing a new string is not nearly the formidable task it may appear to be. Probably the biggest nuisance is the fact that piano wire has the resiliency of spring wire and is difficult to work with, at least until you learn how to handle it properly.

The supply houses have all the wire sizes in 1/4-pound rolls and larger, plus Universal Bass Strings, which come in half sizes to match, or nearly match most any bass string. They also have a flat fiber case especially designed to carry a complete set of Universal Bass Strings, plus small coils of tenor and treble wire, thus equipping the technician for nearly any string replacement problem he may run into.

The following procedures apply to both verticals and grands. Before continuing, however, please re-read the chapter on STRINGS in SECTION 1

TREBLE AND TENOR STRINGS

If the string replacement is to be on a vertical, remove the action and set it aside. Usually the broken wire string is still in the piano so the first thing to do is to turn out the two tuning pins involved, removing them and the old wire from the piano. Next, with the music wire gauge and the bass string and tuning pin gauge, measure the diameter of the old wire and also the diameter size of the tuning pin.

Select the same size wire from one of your coils and two of the next largest size tuning pins. Unwind enough of the wire to reach from one pin hole, down around the hitch pin at the bottom and back to the other pin hole, plus about a foot to spare. Better to have too much than too little, and piano wire is inexpensive.

Put your curved end of the tube string inserter down through the space behind the pressure bar at the exact place where the old string was. Thread the end of the new wire in the curved end of the string inserter and, holding it tight in the inserter, pull the string inserter back through and from under the pressure bar, feeding the new string through as it is removed. Take off the inserter and thread that end of the wire through the hole in the end of the tuning pin and with the chain nose pliers, bend a right-angle about 1/8 inch from the end. Pull the string back until the right-angle stops the string and with the T handle on this tuning pin, turn the pin while you are holding the wire tightly against it untill you have made 2 turns of a coil toward the inside of the pin (the inside is toward the threads). This is important. Push this pin with the wire attached into the hole fartherest to the left and tap it in a little with the butt of your hand on the handle of the T handle.

Run the wire down and around the hitch pin at the bottom, making sure it is around the correct empty one, then run it back up and repeat the procedure with the tube string inserter. When you have this end of the wire under the pressure bar, run it up past the second hole and about 3 & 1/2 inches further, then cut it off with the wire cutters. Thread this end of the wire through the second tuning pin and turn on coils as before. Insert it in the second hole, tap it in slightly, then draw up most of the slack in the wire. Position the wire over both tracks of the bridge pins, using the nearby strings as guides.

Put the tuning pin setter on one of the new pins and with a small hammer, tap in the pin, leaving about 3/8 to 1/2 inch of pin still exposed between the bottom of the last coil and the plate. Never drive in a tuning pin by direct blows from a hammer. It will damage the end of the pin and make it difficult to tune.

Now, pull the newly formed coil together tightly with the coil setter in one hand while pulling up the rest of the slack in the wire with the T handle in the other hand. Use the screwdriver blade to position the strings to their right position and distance apart, near the pressure bar. Pull the new string(s) up in tune, plucking the strings next to it as guides. If you have a string stretcher, use it now. It will help stabilize the new string. Invariably, however, it will be necessary to come back to pull up new strings after a few days or so.

If the broken string is in the tenor section, with access to its hitch and bridge pins inhibited by the bass strings, it may be necessary to loosen a few of the bass strings in order to reach in to position the new wires.

A handy tool here is a Soundboard Steel. This is simply a narrow strip of spring steel, about 1/2 inch wide by 2 feet long, with a slot near one end. This is designed for fishing cloths under the strings of a grand piano to clean the soundboard. However, this also makes a good stringing aid.

After you have estimated the double length to and from the tuning pins, plus a foot or so extra, cut a length of the proper size wire. Place the two ends of the wire together and find the center. Press the wire together at this center until you have made a tight "V". With a length of filament or other strong tape, fasten this V to one end of the soundboard steel. Now you can feed it down and under the bass strings without it becoming tangled. When you have taken off the tape and positioned the V over the hitch pin, clamp a small Vise Grips pliers over the hitch pin to prevent the wire from coming off while you are working with the other ends.

All this seems like a lot to go through, and it is one of the more bothersome jobs in piano work, but after you have done it a few times and gained confidence, it won't bother you.

BASS STRINGS

Compared to lower tenor strings, installing a bass string is a breeze, mainly because they are more easily accessible and because they involve only one tuning pin instead of two.

Find the broken bass string, which is usually in the bottom of the piano, and measure it with the bass string gauge. Place the new and old strings along side each other with the looped ends together and, with the wire cutters, carefully mark the copper winding of the new string where the winding of the old one begins and ends.

If the old string is missing, this will have to be done by sighting sizes of new strings, along side the strings next to the missing one, until an appropriate size is found. This also applies to the length and position of the winding. After you become accustomed to string sizes, you can almost estimate what the needed size will be.

Remove the old tuning pin with the T handle. Place the new bass string in the piano with the loop end over its hitch pin and position it up past the old tuning pin hole. Measure with the width of your hand about 3 & 1/2 or 4 inches past the tuning pin hole and cut off the new string there. Now, take the string out of the piano and with the chain nose pliers, unwind the copper windings at each end of the new string, up to the points where you have marked them. After you have cut off the excess copper, smooth down the remaining ends with the pliers.

Install the string in the piano again and this time position it over both the hitch and bridge pins. Run the top end under any agraffes (on grands) and cut off any excess wire so the end is 3 & 1/2 inches past the tuning pin hole.

Install the next-size-larger tuning pin and make the coil. Tap in and tighten up the coil. Finish driving in to the proper distance and tune up, stretch, re-tune, etc.

Remember not to drive the pin in too far. It is better to have a little too much room between the coil and the plate, than not enough.

A word of caution about old grands. If the string installations are near the center of the piano, it is a good idea to use a pin block jack, installed under the center of the pin block, between the floor of the frame and the pin block. These are small adjustable jacks, with extenders and wooden blocks used to prop up the pinblock to prevent the pounding in of tuning pins from cracking or splitting the old pin block.

It would enhance your image and save you considerable travel time, to carry a complete set of Universal bass strings and several sizes of piano wire in small coils. This will also add to your peace of mind, knowing that you have the materials to replace any broken strings that may occur while tuning old pianos.

It is an accepted rule with piano technicians that they are not responsible for strings that break in the course of a normal tuning. This occurrence is considered to be the fault of the string or the condition of the piano; therefore, string replacement is at the expense of the piano owner. If the piano appears to be a probable case of breaking strings during tuning, make this point of responsibility clear to the owner before beginning the work.

TUNING PIN PROBLEMS
LOOSE TUNING PINS

Actually, there are very few tuning pin problems, as such. The problems are with the pin block that they are in. Sometimes the pin block in older pianos will dry out and shrink with age or from long exposure to a dry environment, or the sides of the pin holes will wear from many tunings over the years.

The ideal solution to loose tuning pins would be to install a new pin block, tuning pins and strings; but the cost of such a major job, unless the piano is a valuable grand, would be extremely impractical.

There are many degrees of loose tuning pins, but if a piano that is not exposed to major changes in humidity and/or temperature will not stay in reasonable tune over a few weeks after a thorough tuning, it needs some doctoring.

One so-called remedy for loose tuning pins is the application of one of various liquids designed to penetrate around the tuning pin into the pin block and swell the tissues of the wood until the tuning pin is "tight" again. The supply houses carry a variety of these tuning pin tighteners, many of which have a glycerine base. In some cases this treatment will improve the situation but after a few months, the tuning pins feel like they are in mush and are loose again. I would not recommend the use of this fluid, except where there is no other alternative.

Sometimes a moderate case of loose tuning pins may be corrected by tapping them in a little further. This can only be done if there is room between the bottom of the coil and the plate. There must be some space here to allow for the coil to expand when the string is pulled up in tuning. If there is not, the string may break when pulled up.

As the vibrations of tapping in tuning pins may cause other loose pins to slip, it is a good idea to first go over all the tuning pins that sound very badly out of tune and test each pin with the tuning lever before beginning to tune the piano. If a pin is loose, make a white mark on top of it with some chalk or a china marker. When you have marked all the loose pins you can find, use the pin setter and a small hammer to tap them in as much as you dare and still leave a little space for coil expansion. This should allow you to complete a reasonably good tuning.

If the tuning pins are too loose for tapping to help, they will have to be replaced with larger pins.

With the T handle, (sometimes called stringing lever), unwind the loose pin about 2 & 1/2 turns and stop. With the tip of a small screwdriver or the point of an awl, pry out the wire from the hole in the tuning pin until it is free of the hole. Now, again with the T handle, completely remove the old tuning pin and lift it out, up through the coil.

Measure the old pin and select one the next size larger and preferably the same length. With the chain-nose pliers, unwind the coil on the string. Try to keep it taut so it will stay in its position on the bridge pins. Cut off the bent end of the wire that was inserted in the tuning pin hole as close to the angle as possible. Insert the wire through the hole in the new tuning pin and make a right-angle bend about 1/8 inch from the end. This is called a becket. Turn the coil on the tuning pin with the T handle you have made about two turns of the coil or until the wire is taut. Make sure the coil is making in the direction toward the threaded end of the pin. Slip the new pin in the hole and tap it in slightly.

Pull up the coil and drive the pin in, using the pin setter and a hammer. Close up the coil with the coil setter and the T handle, then pull it up to pitch with the tuning lever.

If the old tuning pin holes are quite loose and mushy, due to excessive treatment with pinblick liquids, it may be necessary to ream out the holes and install new pins that are two or three sizes larger than the old ones. The piano supply companies have special reamers for each size tuning pin for this purpose. If you decide to do this, be very careful not to over-ream the holes or you will have the same problem when you finish as when you started. It is best to use a variable-speed drill set on medium low. Do not attempt this until you have had some experience in re-pinning.

CRACKED PIN BLOCKS

One of the worst problems to encounter is the cracked pin block. This is identified by a LINE of several tuning pins that are EXTREMELY out of tune and cannot be stabilized when pulled up. This problem is rare but the technician should be able to recognize it. Since little can be done in the home to remedy this situation, explain it to the customer and bow out.

In negative circumstances it is prudent to decline to service certain pianos. The real problems begin when you agree to do work that is unsatisfactory. Avoid no-win situations.

PEDAL AND TRAPWORK REPAIR

The pedals are connected to the action by pivoted horizontal levers, connected to pedal rods, which are 1/2-inch dowels that run vertically to the action. Steel pins in the end of these pedal rods, fit into holes in the pedal levers and action levers. About half-way along their length, these pedal levers are mounted on trap lever springs which are attached to the floor of the piano. The lever end over the pedal is connected to it by long screws with nuts for adjusting the response of the pedals.

Occassionally, it may be necessary to replace a broken trap lever spring or a pedal rod pin that has worked out. In emergencies, a nail with the head cut off will work fine.

Most pedal regulation is a simple matter involving the turning of a nut or two with a small crescent wrench.

Grand trapwork is basically the same as the vertical but the rods are much shorter and the connectors are different. Working on grand trapwork is inconvenient, as it must be done while lying on the back, and removing the action for accessibility is sometimes necessary.

The grand pedal lyre, along with its braces, unscrews from the underside of the keybed, for repair or moving the piano.

Regulating pedal response on grands is usually done by adjusters on the pedal rods which are located on the back side of the lyre.

A properly regulated sustain pedal should begin to lift the dampers when it is depressed 1/3 of the way.

HINGES AND CASTERS

There are various sizes of hinges used on pianos, all of which are available at the supply houses. Missing hinges are rare but the hinge pins are sometimes missing. Carry a few assorted sizes of nails to use as hinge pin replacements so you can prop up piano lids for tuning, etc.

On a few modern spinets and consoles, the lid is hinged at one end and must be removed for tuning. This is best done by removing the hinge pin(s). If they are in too tight, tap them out, using the center pin punch and a small hammer.

Casters are an unusual problem as the technician seldom moves pianos about for tuning or small repairs. Of course, a wide variety of casters is available from the supply houses.

Installing casters with sockets on a vertical usually involves laying the piano on its back. It is best to have some help for this. Also, put down two short lengths of 2 by 4 where the top of the back will rest, so there will be a space to put the hands when setting it upright again.

To install casters on grands, use a padded saw horse or similar object to prop up the frame by each leg so you can remove the legs, one at a time, to install the new caster. Most grand legs have two large screws that go up through the leg wings. After removing these, slide the top of the leg toward the piano to disengage the leg plates.

....

Section 3. Regulation

REGULATING TOOLS
Top: L to R.
Technician's Screwdriver
Small Screwdriver
Button Regulator
2 Pointed Capstan Regulators
2 Capstan Screw Wrenches
Damper Regulator
Letoff Regulating Screwdriver
Key Spacer
Backcheck Regulator
String Height Gage
Combination Handle

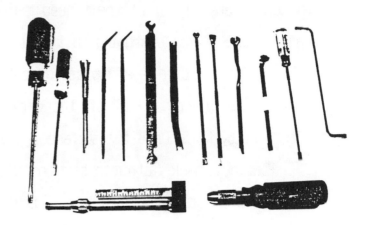

REGULATING THE VERTICAL ACTION

Proper regulation cannot be done until any needed repair has been completed and the action screws checked for tightness.

Regulating specifications vary slightly with each piano manufacturer. However, the procedures given here should work nicely in most cases and slight modifications, at the discretion of the technician, should take care of the rest.

STEP 1. SPACE HAMMERS

Space the hammers so they will squarely strike all the strings in the unison that they are intended to strike. Hammers may be moved a little to the right or left by loosening the hammer butt flange screw and holding the hammer in the desired direction, while re-tightening the screw.

69

STEP 2. INSTALL UNDERFELTS

Remove the action and keys, as described earlier. Inspect the underfelts to see if any or all of them need replacing. Clean the keybed with a hose vacuum and if you are going to install new underfelts, suck up the old balance rail and front rail felts and paper punchings, aided by a screwdriver for pushing them up on the pins. Pull off the back rail cloth and scrape off the old glue with a putty knife until the surface is level and smooth.

Cut new back rail cloth sections, the same thickness as the old, and glue in place where the old cloth was. This Key Cloth is available in rolls.

Take two adjoining white keys from each end of the key set and two adjoining keys from the center of the set. Put the felt balance rail and front rail punchings over the key pins for these keys and put these keys in place on the keybed.

Check the key height. This is done by holding the keys down in the back, (lay a book or something on the back half of the keys) and measuring with a small rule at the front of the key, from the keybed to the top of the key top. This measurement varies with different pianos but should be about 2 & 1/2 inches, give or take 1/8 inch. Whatever figure you decide on, insert paper balance rail punchings under the keys till all the keys you have in place are the same height.

At the two keys on the left, place the key dip block on top of the left key and press it down with one hand, while holding the _back_ of the other key down, so its front is in the up position. If the top of the up key is even with the top of the key dip block, the key "dip" or distance it travels when depressed is correct. This should be 3/8 inch.

If the key top is _above_ the top of the key dip block, remove the   key and balance rail felt and add a paper balance rail punching of the appropriate thickness, then replace the balance rail felt and key and test again. If OK, do the adjoining key. Repeat this procedure with the keys on the other two sections.

If the key top is <u>below</u> the top of the key dip block, remove the key and the <u>front</u> felt punching and put a front rail paper or cardboard punching of the appropriate thickness over the pin and replace the felt and key. If OK, do the adjoining key and repeat this procedure with the keys on the other two sections.

When you have determined with the test keys which addition of paper punchings arrives at the proper key dip, put these punchings on the rest of the front and balance rail pins, then add the felts. Replace all the keys and the action and bolt in place.

STEP 3. SET HAMMER TRAVEL

Check the hammer travel distance. This is the distance from the strings to the face of the hammer while at rest, (in the unplayed position). If you intend to file the hammers, do that before proceeding.

The hammer blow or hammer travel distance should be 1 & 3/4 inches. If it is too much, glue a front rail punching or two in each of the four places under the front of the hammer rest rail. If the distance is too short, remove some of the felt already there until the distance is correct.

STEP 4. REMOVE LOST MOTION

Lost motion is the slack in an action unit. Its elimination is essential to proper action response. When the finger begins to depress the key, the hammer should start to move toward the strings.

To take out lost motion, turn the capstan screw at the back of the key. This is usually accomplished with either a capstan wrench or a round capstan regulator, depending on the piano. Some spinets have "buttons" at the back end of the keys, through which the sticker wires screw into. These may be turned with the fingers of a drop action button regulator that fits into the combination handle.

Turn these screws until there is no loose play in the action units when the key is touched lightly. If the hammer rises from the hammer rest rail, you have turned the capstan too far.

STEP 5. LEVEL THE KEYS

Leveling the keys is a rather tedious task and involves the developing of a certain intuition as to which paper balance rail punching to use without trial and error. These paper and cardboard washers are color-coded to identify their thickness, which ranges from .002 inches to .045 inches. These are quite inexpensive but a plastic compartment box of the assorted sizes is mandatory for key leveling.

Use your three sets of two guide keys that you have already leveled to sight the other keys. Using a straight edge can be of help. Remove each white key and add or subtract the necessary paper balance rail puchings until all the white keys are level.

When all the whites are level, check three sets of these; two adjoining black keys on the far left, in the center and on the far right. Take these measurements when both the black and white keys involved are in the rest, or up position. Measure from the top of the adjoining white key to the top of the black key, at the front, just before the slope of the black key begins. The measurement should be 1/2 inch. Add or take out balance rail paper punchings till all your guide keys are at this measurement. Now, using the guide keys to sight by, level the rest of the black keys. Again, a straight edge may help.

STEP 6. REGULATE THE LET-OFF

The let-off is the point where the jack disengages or kicks out from under the hammer butt. This allows the hammer to strike the string and rebound on its own momentum.

Let-off is controlled by the looped regulating screw located behind the jack. It goes through the let-off rail and into the let-off button, which can be moved up and down by turning the let-off regulating screw with the let-off regulating screwdriver that fits in the combination handle. Let-off on verticals should be 1/8 inch. Acquire a piece of wood or aluminum, about 12 inches by 2 inches, and exactly 1/8-inch thick. Attach this with a little masking tape, across the strings in the path of the hammer blows to be regulated. Turn the let-off regulating screw with the regulating screwdriver so the jack will release right at the point where it touches your strip. Do this all along the complete action. It will give you an exact 1/8-inch let-off regulation job.

STEP 7. REGULATE BACKCHECKS

Regulate the backchecks. Re-check your guide white keys on both ends and in the center with the key dip block, to make certain they have the proper dip. Bend the backcheck wires so the catchers on these units will stop the hammer's rebound after the hammer has retracted 5/8 inch from the string. Use these guides to bend the other backcheck wires accordingly. On some old pianos where the felts are worn, individual testing for the 5/8-inch stopping position may be required.

STEP 8. REGULATE THE DAMPERS

Regulating the dampers: Bend the damper wires with one of the damper regulators that fit into the combination handle, so each damper is in line with all the strings of each unison. Play each key that has a damper and make sure the damper seats properly and cuts off all of the sound when the key is released.

On old pianos, the damper felts dry out and become depressed and dirty, causing an after-sound when they touch the strings when the key is released. Dampers in this condition should be replaced.

Dampers should begin lifting when the key is half depressed, or 3/16 inch. It may be necessary to remove the action to check the spoons that lift the damper levers. They should all be a uniform height and any that are too high or too low will be obvious by the raised or lowered bottom ends of the damper levers. To align, bend with one of the damper regulators and re-install the action.

Go over the dampers where you bent the spoons and re-adjust the damper wires so they will lift at 3/16-inch like the rest.

STEP 9. LAY THE TOUCH

Most of this operation you have already done in steps 2 and 5 but go over the white keys with the key dip block and check for the proper dip again. Just behind the sharp of the black keys, the top of the wood should be about half way up the white key top. To check the dip of the black keys, press a black key, and the white keys on either side of it, down at the same time. if the back of all three keys is the same height, the sharp has the proper dip. If the sharp is higher, add the appropriate front rail paper or cardboard punching(s). If it is lower, take out some.

STEP 10. SET THE AFTER-TOUCH

After-touch is the "feel" of the keys. It is the minute distance the key travels after the let-off and before it reaches bottom. This distance is approximately .030 inches. Without after-touch, the hammers would bobble but it must be very slight and barely perceptible to the player.

If you have properly done all of the steps so far, most of the keys probably already have the proper after-touch. A good way to check or to set after-touch is to make a small device for this purpose. Take a standard 3 X 5 file card. Starting at one end, using a ruler and pencil, make three lines from side to side, exactly 3/4-inch apart. Fold the card at the first two lines with a hard fold and with scissors, cut it off at the third line. You should have a three-layered, 3-inch long flat piece. With the scissors, cut a notch in the center of one end, about 3/16-inch wide and 1/2-inch long.

To check or set the after-touch, slip the notched end around the front rail key pin, on top of the felt punching, and press the key on top of it. If, when you press the key down <u>hard</u>, the let-off trips, the after-touch is correct. If the let-off does not trip, remove some of the front rail card or paper punchings. If there is too much after-touch, add punchings. Do this with all the keys.

This completes the vertical regulation. Though it seems like a lot to do, with practice and experience, it can be done in one session, plus tuning.

Go through these procedures in the order they are given or you may waste considerable time and still not arrive at a satisfactory result. A good regulation job is something to be proud of.

AVERAGE MEASUREMENTS FOR VERTICAL ACTION REGULATING

Key height	= 2 & 1/2 in.
Hammer blow	= 1 & 3/4 in.
Hammer let-off	= 1/8 in.
Key dip	= 3/8 in.
Backckeck	= 5/8 in.

....

REGULATING THE GRAND ACTION

Unlike vertical piano regulation, which must be done with the action in the piano, a grand action may be taken to the shop for a complete regulation job. This is accomplished with the use of a String Height Gauge and a Grand Regulating Rack.

The string height gauge is a small self-adjusting device that is set in the keybed of the grand, after the action has been removed. Beginning with the bass and working from left to right, it is placed under the left, then the right string or string unisons of each section of strings, then its spring is released so the top of its post is up against the string(s). A knob is tightened and the gauge removed. The correct heights from a scale along its side are written down and used later to set the grand regulating rack.

The regulating rack consists of two adjustable posts with connecting cross beams. It is set on the work bench, just behind the hammers on the grand action, one section at a time. The readings obtained from the string height gauge are used to set the height of the top beam of the rack, thus simulating the strings of the piano. In this way the various measurements for regulation can be checked and corrected without the tiring tedium of having to remove and return the action in the piano every time an adjustment is made. A perfectly level surface, measuring about 4 & 1/2 X 2 & 1/2 feet is required to use the regulating rack with the grand action.

STEP 1. CLEAN THE KEYBED

Remove the grand action and clean the keybed. If the floor of the keybed is rough, sand it with a medium sandpaper and apply some silicone spray so the action will slide easily when the left pedal is pressed.

This is also a good time to clean the soundboard with the soundboard steel and clean the strings. There are special hard rubber erasers, impregnated with an abrasive, available for this purpose.

STEP 2. LEVEL THE KEY FRAME

Remove the action from the key frame by taking out the 10 or 12 screws from the legs of the action brackets. Remove the key stop rail and remove all the keys from the key frame. Be sure to keep them in order. Put the key frame back in the keybed and refasten the key frame blocks (if any) at the ends of the keybed.

With your fingers, tap around the keybed, especially at the corners and the center of the rails and listen for any knocks that indicate there is space between the key frame and the keybed. If any is detected, turn down the key frame regulating screw at this point, a very little at a time, until the knock is removed. When all knocks are gone, the keyframe may be considered level. Remove the key frame from the keybed.

STEP 3. CHECK WIPPEN FELTS

Tie a length of cord over the hammer shanks so as to fasten each section down to the hammer rest rail. Carefully turn the action over on a flat surface or mount it in an action cradle. Inspect the felts on the bottom of the wippens to see if they are badly indented by the heads of the capstan screws. If they are, they will have to be replaced as a good regulation with indented wippen felts is virtually impossible.

If some or all of the wippen felts need replacing, wet the surface of the old felts liberally with household ammonia, using a plastic dispenser, eyedropper, or equivalent. Do not spill it down in the action. After a few minutes, the old felts can be removed with the tip of a knife. Clean off the old glue and ammonia, etc. from the wood and let dry.

Cut the required number of felts, the same length as the old ones, from a roll of action cloth, which is already the correct width. A guillotine-type felt cutter saves a lot of time when cutting many felts of the same size.

Apply contact cement to both the bottom of the flange and one side of the action cloth. Let dry a few minutes and carefully stick together.

STEP 4. CHECK UNDERFELTS

Check and replace any or all underfelts, as needed. Follow the same procedures described in Step 2 of Regulating The Vertical Action.

STEP 5. EASE THE KEYS

Put the keys back on the keyframe and check to see if they all work easily but without undue sideplay, which should just be perceptible when the key is moved from side to side with the fingers when in a down position.

STEP 6. LEVEL THE KEYS

Leveling the keys on a grand key frame is done without the action in place and so requires weights on the back end of the keys to simulate the weight of the action unit on each key. These are called Grand Key Leveling Leads and have clips to hook them over the backchecks at the back of the keys. They are available in sets.

Clip the weights on all the white keys, then proceed with the leveling process as described in Step 5 of Regulating The Vertical Action.

When all the white keys are level, put weights on the black keys, a section at a time, leaving the weights on the white keys of that section. Level these sharps acording to instructions in Step 5 of Regulating The Vertical Action.

STEP 7. SET THE DIP

Most of this step has probably already been accomplished in Step 4. Check the white keys again for the proper 3/8-inch dip. Correct if necessary with paper or card front rail punchings.

As with the vertical, the wood of the sharp key, just behind the sharp should be about half way between the bottom and top of the white key top. Press the black key and the two adjoining white keys down simultaneously and check to see that the backs of the three keys are level together. If not, rectify with punchings.

The sharp should be 1/2 inch above the white keys, at a point just behind the slope, when all three keys are in the up position. When a black key is depressed, its top should the 1/8 inch above the white keys when the white keys are in the up position.

STEP 8. CHECK CENTERS & TIGHTEN SCREWS

Make sure the jacks, the cradle and the wippen flange move freely and without side-wobble. If too tight, treat with center pin lube. If too loose, re-pin with larger size. Also, jacks should not rub the sides of the cradle. If necessary, use sandpaper to reduce the rubbing side of the jack a little and lubricate with silicone or paraffin. Tighten the wippen flange screws.

STEP 9. SET HAMMER HEIGHT

With the the appropriate capstan wrench, turn up the capstans one turn. Replace the action on the key frame and re-insert and tighten screws.

Set the grand regulating rack over the bass section and set its top bar to the height indicated for that section from the measurements previously taken with the string height gauge.

with the proper capstan wrench, turn the capstan screw at the left side of the bass section until the hammer is 1 & 7/8 inches from the simulated string. (Some makes of pianos use a 1 & 3/4-inch measurement.) Now do the same with the hammer on the far right of the section. Adjust the capstans of the other keys so the hammers in this section are all the same height. Unlike the verticals, the hammers of grands do not rest on the hammer rest rail but should be 1/8 inch from this rail when at rest. To achieve this, it may sometimes be necessary to lower the hammer rest rail.

Repeat this operation with each section, working to the right, and using the appropriate measurements for each section until all the hammers in that section are level with one another in that section. Of course, the bass hammers will be higher due to the bass over-stringing.

STEM 10. SPACE THE REPETITIONS

Make sure the repetition is in line with the hammer and that the jack is squarely under the knuckle of the hammer assembly. If it leans to one side, remove the wippen flange and, using thin strips of masking tape, stick on one or more shims in the groove of the flange between the side and the screw hole. Put these on the side <u>opposite</u> the direction the repetition is leaning. The correct number of shims will bring it in line.

STEP 11. ADJUST JACK POSITION

Adjust the jack regulating screw (accessible from the key side of the action) with a grand drop screw regulator so that the back of the jack is in line with the back of the knuckle strip. (The term back refers to the direction away from the keyboard.) Do this to all jacks.

STEP 12. SET THE REPETITION HEIGHT

Turn the repetition lever regulating screw (on top of and near the back of the wippen assembly) so the top of the jack is just below the top of the cradle (the arm that rocks up and down). This can best be done by feel as it should be barely below the cradle top. Repeat this procedure with all repetitions.

STEP 13. REGULATE THE LET–OFF

Before regulating the let–off it may first be necessary to turn down the drop screws, located on top of the hammer shank near the flange.

Using the grand regulating rack, turn the let–off screw, found in the let–off rail on the keyboard side of the action, so the hammer lets off a scant 1/16 inch from the "string". Do this to all hammers in all sections.

STEP 14. REGULATE THE REPETITION SPRINGS

Turn the repetition spring tension screw, located near the back of the rocker arm, so the tension is such that when the key is depressed and slowly released, the repetition should throw the hammer upward. This upward movement should be smooth, not jumpy. Repeat with all units.

Different makes of pianos may require slightly different tools for this operation; some, small screwdrivers; others, the slotted regulating tool or a spring bender.

STEP 15. REGULATE THE DROP SCREWS

Turn the drop screw on top of the hammer butt with a small screwdriver or the slotted regulating tool so the hammer will drop another 1/8 inch after its 1/16 inch let–off drop. Do this to all units.

STEP 16. LAY THE TOUCH AND AFTER–TOUCH

This is done according to the instructions in Steps 9 and 10 of Regulating The Vertical Action. The only difference here is that the after–touch of a grand is slightly more than the verticals. To allow for this, make 6 folds in a 3 X 5 card (instead of 3) and use as an after–touch gauge.

STEP 17. REGULATE BACKCHECKS

Still using the regulating rack, bend the backchecck wires so the hammers are caught and check at 5/8-inch from the string. Repeat this with all backchecks.

STEP 18. RE-CHECK THE REPETITION SPRINGS

Go over the action and press each key and slowly let it up, to check the even upward thrust of the hammer when the key is released.

Put the action back in the piano and play all the keys to be sure they are all working properly. Complete the job with whatever adjustments are necessary.

As with the verticals, grand action regulation should be performed in the order given so as not to "undo" any of the steps already completed.

When you have successfully completed a grand action regulation, you are to be congratulated, as it is one of the most complex tasks required of a piano technician and also one that many technicians try to avoid. When you have completed this hurdle, you are well on your way.

....

REGULATING THE GRAND DAMPERS

Replacing the grand dampers is covered in the previous section of that title. Note that dampers are omitted in the upper treble of pianos.

Grand dampers seldom require regulation. When the action is returned to the piano and tested after regulation and the dampers perform properly, leave them alone. If they do not operate properly, note the following procedures:

If the dampers do not seat properly on the strings, allowing sound to leak through, bend the damper wires slightly to correct this problem.

Following are some measurements that will aid in grand damper regulation:

The sustaining pedal should begin to lift the damper when it is depressed 1/3 of the way down. Also, the dampers should begin to lift when the key is depressed 1/3rd.

To allow the damper to follow the vibrating string, the damper lever should not reach its bottom by 1/16 inch, when at rest.

The damper stop rail should be regulated so the dampers can be lifted another 1/8 inch, after the complete pedal lift.

The "soft" pedal should move the keys to the right, just enough to clear the left string of the three-string treble unisons.

The sostenuto lever should be 1/16 inch under the lips when the middle pedal is depressed – and 1/16 inch in the clear when that pedal is at rest.

To check the sostenuto, press the sustaining (right) pedal and, while holding it down, press the sostenuto (middle) pedal and hold it down. Now release the sustaining pedal while still holding down the sostenuto. All the dampers should remain up. The ones that do not need regulating. Keep in mind that on some pianos, the sostenuto does not affect the entire range of dampers.

Occasionally, especially after moving, the short dowels that convey the pedal/trap movement up through the floor of the piano to the damper mechnaisms may be missing. If so, they will have to be replaced. You may have to measure and experiment a little to find the proper lengths for the new 1/2-inch dowels.

Sometimes the felts that are either on the back of the keys or on the underside of the damper levers, may require changing to felts of greater or lesser thickness, in order to arrive at the desired damper response.

VOICING

Voicing or tone regulation involves the shape and density of the hammer felt. (Re-read the section on Hammers.) In time, the striking surface of the pear-shaped hammer becomes compacted, grooved and flat from its contact with the steel strings. This condition affects the tones produced, making them sound tubby or tinny.

FILING

To remedy this situation, the hammers must be filed to return them to their original contour. This is done with a Sandpaper File and hammers are carefully re-contoured by filing on their top and bottom, in a direction toward the striking point, but not on the striking point, and ninety degrees from the sides. Remember, the hammer must strike its group of strings squarely, hitting all of them at the same time. Do not remove any more felt than necessary.

In the case of verticals, this process can be done while the action is still in the piano. Of course, the grand action must be removed. If you intend to regulate an action, do any hammer filing first. If no regulation is planned, it still may be necessary to regulate the let-offs, since the wear, plus filing, would cause the let-off to occur too soon.

NEEDLING

To relieve the hardness and density of hammers, they are pierced with the needles of the Voicing Tool. These tools come in a variety of sizes and usually hold four small needles which are removable. By removing two of the needles and working with just two, pierce the hammer a few times from the top and the bottom, just behind the striking face and pointing the needles toward the center of the hammer. Never needle the striking surface as this would cause rapid hammer deteoriation. Needle just a little at a time and test for its sound. Over-needling will make the hammer sound weak and mushy. Some technicians push the needles through the sides of the hammer, about 1/4 inch back from the striking surface.

After a new set of hammers has been installed and all necessary repair and regulation has been done, plus the tuning, the hammers should be gone over with the voicing tool. The object is to have the sound caused by the hammer impact, uniform in graduated density. Again, do not over-needle.

DOPING

If hammers are too soft, the supply houses have a hammer felt hardener that is made with lacquer. This process is sometimes called "doping" the hammers. This fluid may be applied to the same areas that would be needled with the voicing tool. This also should not be applied directly to the striking surface. This process is sometimes referred to as "doping" the hammers.

The ultimate sound reached by tone regulation is of course up to the quality, condition and age of the instrument and the conceptual ear of the technician. If in doubt when tone regulating, find a note on the piano where the hammer has the quality that appeals to your ear, then try to get the other hammers to match it.

....

Section 4. Tuning

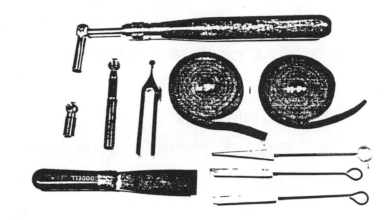

TUNING TOOLS
Top: Adjustable Tuning Lever
Second Row: L to R.
Short Lever Tip
Long Lever Tip w/Extension
2 Felt Strip Mutes
Bottom:
Putty Knife (Stp. Mute Inserter)
1 Double & 2 Single Stick Mutes

PIANO TUNING

The process of tuning musical instruments could be one of man's oldest sciences. Ever since he began to pound on hollow logs and drums to communicate, or express himself by blowing through hollow reeds, the different sounds he could make were important to him and probably were evolved along with the development of language.

Piano tuning in essence is regulating the tension of the piano's strings so the sounds they produce will be "in order". Without properly tuned pianos and other compatibly tuned musical instruments, music as we know it today, would be impossible.

While the piano is thought of by many as a solo instrument, it must be remembered that pianos are also used in large part to accompany vocalists, with vocal groups, orchestras and with symphony orchestras by concert pianists.

The performance and reputation of a professional artist depends on the piano technician to lay the foundation for a successful engagement.

TOOLS

Only a few tools are needed in the tuning process. They are: the tuning lever (often called tuning hammer), tuning fork, several rubber stick mutes, several felt strip mutes, an extension tuning lever head for grands, and a narrow putty knife for inserting the felt strip mutes.

THE TUNING LEVER

Tuning is the name of the game and the tuning lever is your most important tool. If you are going to get into tuning seriously, by all means get a good lever, preferably one with an extension handle. These are very well made and will last a lifetime. The heads and tips are replaceable and interchangeable and come in a variety of sizes, angles and lengths. A #3 star tip is recommended.

Do not attempt serious tuning with one of the so-called "student" models. They are too light and flexible for accurate tuning.

MUTES

Strings can only be tuned one at a time, so mutes are used to prevent the strings of the unison that are not being tuned or listened to, from vibrating. Without mutes, tuning would be almost impossible.

There are many types and sizes of mutes but the type most commonly used is the stick mute, which is made of a rubber wedge, impaled on a wire handle. About four of these is sufficient. For great help at the end of sections, a wide wedge may be easily made by gluing with contact cement, a wedge mute without the handle, to the side of another wedge mute with the wire handle.

You will need about six felt strip mutes of varying thicknesses and with a slight taper at one end. These are about 50 inches long.

The putty knife is used as an aid in inserting the felt strip between the unisons. Some technicians use a screwdriver or the handle of a stick mute. The putty knife works better.

THE TUNING FORK

The tuning fork, of course, is to give the tuner a reference pitch. Though A-440 is the standard term used in reference to pitch, most technicians use a C-523.3 fork. This is the C above Middle C (C-5) and is relative to A-440.

THE EXTENSION HEAD

The extension head is used in the tuning of the top treble section of a grand piano to raise the handle of the tuning lever above the side of the case so it can be more easily manipulated. This, like the other heads, quickly screws on and off the tuning lever shaft.

USING THE TUNING TOOLS

TUNER'S POSITION AT THE PIANO

Spinets, consoles and grands are tuned in the sitting position, while uprights are tuned while standing. In either case, the tuner is facing the piano with both feet flat on the floor, the right hand on the tuning lever and the left hand on the keyboard.

NOTE: Throughout this text we will be assuming the student is right-handed. However, there are many excellent left-handed tuners, and some say this position is better. In any case, for those lefties, just reverse the descriptions for the right and left hands. In some situations, you will be pushing instead of pulling.

POSITION OF THE TUNING LEVER

Imagine the tuning lever is the hour hand of a clock; the metal tip is the hub in the center of the clock and the handle is the hour hand. The lever tip should always be placed solidly on the tuning pin, handle up. For verticals, the lever position should be from 12 to 2 o'clock – for grands, from 1 to 3 o'clock.

HAND POSITION 1.

Place the right hand on the tuning lever with the palm open and the fingers curled around the end of the handle, the thumb braced against the handle and pointing down toward the metal head. This position offers the best control for pulling. Remember, most movements made with the tuning lever are very slight.

HAND POSITION 2.

With the back of the hand toward the strings, make a loose fist over the end of the tuning lever, the thumb on the end of the handle. This position is essential when fine tuning and setting the tuning pin.

The process of tuning involves the rapid changing back and forth of these positions.

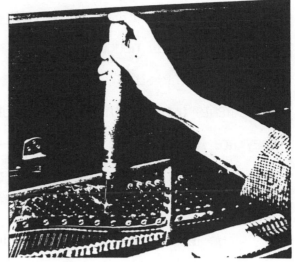

HAND POSITIONS ON THE TUNING LEVER

Top Left: Hand Position No. 1 for verticals.

Top Right: Position No. 2.

Bottom Left: Hand Position No. 1 for grands.

Bottom Right: Position No. 2.

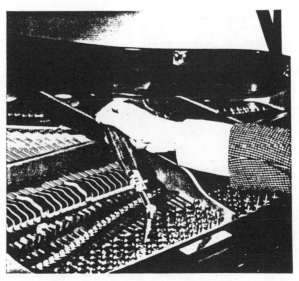

LEVER MOVEMENTS

Aside from drastic pitch raising, the movements of the tuning lever are confined to small nudges and tugs.

After the string is put in the vicinity of where it is to be "set", the movements used by the tuner to put it where he wants it are almost quivers. they are like //////// rather than ————. The string is minutely jockeyed back and forth until it is in place - in relation to the string to which it is being tuned.

The lever should always move in an arc, level with the same plane as the plate and the pin block. Never attempt to twist the tuning pin up or down away from this level movement as it may bend the pin or damage the pinblock and cause tuning problems later.

USING THE MUTES

There are several ways of using mutes in tuning and it is eventually up to the individual tuner to decide on which muting system is best for him. In this course, however, we will be using the total muting system; that is, muting off all the side strings of the unisons before beginning to tune the piano. This system saves time and the bother of moving several stick mutes around during tuning. This will be taken up later, after the initial practice of getting used to the tools, the sounds and the procedures.

USING THE STRIP MUTES

With the putty knife, loops of the strip mute are pushed between the 3 string unisons of the tenor and treble sections, leaving enough loop over the unmuted center string to allow it to sound and vibrate freely. In the upper tenor ssection, where the thin end of the strip mute is inserted, it is necessary to push the mute up with the fingers, out of the way of the hammer's path. In the lower treble, after the strip mute has been inserted between the strings, carefully pull out the dampers in groups of threes or fours with one hand and just as carefully, push the strip mute down behind the damper felts, then release the dampers. This clears the way for the hammers to strike.

In the bass section, (working from right to left) the strip mute is inserted between the 2-string unisons on <u>every other</u> unison. To simplify this, just push the mute in between the 2nd and 3rd string (L to R), then count 4 strings, insert mute, count 4 strings, insert mute, etc.

After you have tuned a while, total muting will become second nature. An experienced tuner can strip-mute a whole piano in about a minute.

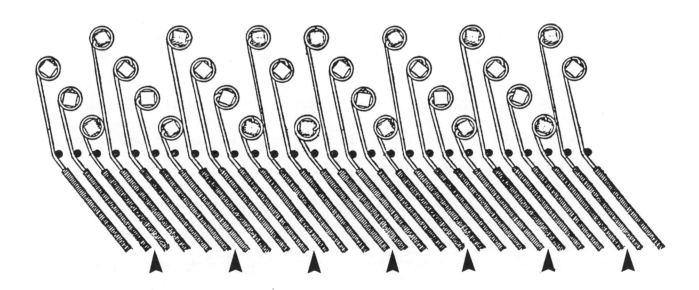

Above: STRIP MUTING THE BASS STRING UNISONS
Push in loops of strip mute at arrows.

USING STICK MUTES

After the temperament octave is set and the octaves tuned, the tuner removes the strip mute from the bass section and, putting the lever on every other 2-unison pin, tunes the bass. He then proceeds to the tenor section, tunes the first left unison and begins to pull out the felt strip, one loop at a time as he tunes. When he gets to the string on the right of a unison, he inserts a stick mute between the <u>left</u> string and the next left unison. this is to give him a clearer sound with the center string and the right one which he is tuning. This procedure is repeated on through the tenor section.

In the treble, after the octaves have been tuned, because of a lack of space, the strip mute is removed and a stick mute is used, first on the right side of the unison while the left string is being tuned to the center one, then on the left side of the unison, while the right string is tuned to the center.

Stick mutes are also used in checking the final tuning job.

USING THE TUNING FORK

Hold the tuning fork by its handle at the bottom of the two tines with the thumb and forefinger of the left hand and strike it on the knee. Now use the bottom of the fork handle to press down and sound Middle C on the piano. This will cause the sound of the fork to be amplified so it can more easily be heard and compared to the C. This method also leaves the right hand free for moving the tuning lever. The fork may be placed on the piano case, or any hard surface to make it resonate after it is struck on the knee, but then it is difficult to hold the fork, play the key, and use the tuning lever at the same time. Never strike a tuning fork on a hard surface as this may permanently impair its accuracy.

TRAINING THE EAR

SOUND AND PITCH

Many may recall from high school physics the demonstration of the turned-on electric buzzer placed under the Bell jar and then the air pumped out, causing the sound of the buzzer to gradually weaken until it was no longer audible, still the clapper could be observed in motion. This proved there must be air for sound to be heard. Also, most everyone has watched the concentric waves produced by throwing a stone into a quiet pool of water. The waves spread outward getting wider and more shallow as they go. If sound could be seen, this same pattern could be observed.

When a piano string is set in motion by the hammer blow, it begins to vibrate at a certain number of vibrations or cycles per second. This number is governed by its length, its density (thickness) and its tension.

Musical tones differ from one another in five ways; pitch, intensity, duration, timbre and resonance. The one with which we will be most concerned in the process of tuning is pitch.

Pitch is the level of frequency, or the highness or lowness of a tone. It is measured by the number of vibrations per second and is indicated variously as: vibrations per second (vps), cycles per second (cps), or hertz (Hz), the modern term for the other two. Since they all mean the same thing, we will use cps in this text.

The approximate range of the human ear lies between 20 and 20,000 cps and the range of the piano is 27.5 cps fpr the lowest bass note and 4186. cps for the highest treble note.

PITCH AND TUNING FORKS

During the Renaissance period in Europe (14th through 18th centuries) pitch was a loosely applied term and "reference tones" were left up to individual communities. Musical historians have discovered over 300 different pitches were in use during that period. To add to this confusion, there were also three general levels of pitch in use; one for church music (both organ and choral), another for orchestras and still another for brass bands.

Coincidental with the invention of the piano, John Shore, an Englishman and court trumpeter to George I, invented the tuning fork in 1711. This is a small steel instrument that, when activated, produces a single pitch with great accuracy and little or no harmonics or overtones.

Attempts to standardize pitch did not become serious until much later. In the United States in the 1880s there was the Steinway or "concert pitch": A-458.cps. At the Vienna Conference in 1885, A-435 became "international pitch". In 1917, the American Federation of Musicians adopted A-440, which was also adopted by the U.S.Bureau of Standards in 1920. The British Standard Institution Conference in 1938, recommended "An Internationally Standard Tuning Frequency of A-440." This is our present tuning standard. All references to A, in regard to pitch and tuning forks, means A above Middle C (A-4).

Tuning forks are available in many tones and pitches but the one most used by piano tuners is C-523.3 (comparative to A-440).

Temperature variation has a slight effect on tuning forks and they are intended to be used at 65 degrees F. A higher temperature causes the pitch to go slightly flat, while a low temperature will make it sharp.

To avoid damaging the accuracy of the tuning fork, it should never be struck on a hard surface. To activate the fork, it should be struck on a padded surface. Most tuners use their knee, which is ideal for this purpose.

Without a pitch standard, music performance would be chaotic as most live performance involves travel from city to city. The problem could be especially troublesome in the broadcast and classical fields where vocalists and instrumentalists perform with continually different orchestras.

Today, pitch in the industrialized world is pretty much standardized at A-440. Notable exception is the pop recording industry where the speed (and pitch) of a recording may be slightly altered for effect, before it is marketed.

WHAT IS "OUT OF TUNE"?

When applied to a piano, out of tune is a general term that actually means the instrument is suffering from either one, two or all three of the following conditions: 1. The unisons are out of sync: 2. The intervals are uneven: and 3. The pitch has dropped unevenly. Usually, these three problems go hand in hand, especially if the piano has not been tuned in some time.

TIME CONCEPTION

Unless they are in some technical field, most persons take a unit of time as small as a second for granted. It is important that the student tuner get a good idea of the length of a second so he can count and compare beats.

A watch or a clock with a second hand will do, but one with a digital second indicator is ideal. Observe the second indicator as it moves and as each second changes, count "one thousand, two thousand, three thousand," etc. up to ten, then repeat. Do this for two full minutes or until a good "feel" for the length of a second is retained.

HEARING BEATS

Excepting piano tuners, it is a rare person indeed who is consciously aware of beats. This is an area where some students may have a little difficulty at first; but this problem will soon pass.

Try to picture in the mind's eye, a clock with a pendulum on the bottom, swinging back-and-forth. The speed of this pendulum can be regulated faster or slower but at the moment it is slowly swinging at one back and forth swing per second. Hear the tick or pulse of the "clock" as it swings and listen for the <u>bottom</u> of the sound. Recall this image when tuning unisons and intervals, and remember to listen to the <u>bottom</u> of the sound for the beats.

When the expression "counting beats" is used, it does not actually mean <u>counting</u> beats per second; as beat rates may sometimes be so fast as to make this impossible. Rather than counting, it is more like <u>comparing</u> beat rates of one string or interval with another, in order to get them slower, faster or the same. Of course, unisons and octaves should be beatless.

MEASUREMENTS

Though it is not necessary to be able to play the piano to be a good tuner, a little basic knowledge of musical theory is essential in describing the tuning process.

INTERVALS

Music and the piano keyboard is divided into half steps or "half-tones". Playing each white and black key in succession, going in one direction, either up or down, produces a chromatic scale. If every <u>other</u> note is played, omitting the note in between, a whole-tone scale is produced. Combinations of whole and half tones make up the major and minor scales.

An interval is the difference in pitch between two notes, sounded at the same time. Intervals derive their names from their position in the scale. The intervals most used in piano tuning are:

Abbreviation:	Name of interval
m3	minor third
3rd	Major third
4th	fourth
5th	fifth
6th	sixth
Maj7th	Major seventh
oct.	octave
10th	tenth

These intervals are used in setting the tones in the temperament octave. This is the octave from F to F around middle C, from which the tuning of the rest of the piano radiates and is based. The intervals are also used as checks, to verify the accuracy of the tuning as it progresses. Tuning is not done "by ear" in the sense that it is guesswork. Become familiar with these intervals and commit them to memory as most of them will be used in every tuning.

BEATS

Probably the great granddaddy of instrument tuning is Pythagores, who, in the 4th century B.C., discovered the phenomenon of vibrations caused by out-of-phase (out-of-tune) intervals, which would gradually disappear as the interval was brought to its perfect state.

When a perfect, in-tune interval of a fourth, fifth or octave is slowly contracted or expanded, making it out of phase (out-of-tune), a pulsating sound called "beats" can be heard. As the interval is contracted or expanded still more, these beats grow faster and faster.

It is the recognition and the ability to compare these beats that make accurate piano tuning possible. A beat is the tuner's name for one vibration or cycle.

It may take a little time to get the ear accustomed to recognizing beats as many people are not aware they exist.

WAVES

A wave is a very slow beat; one that takes longer than one second of time to repeat.

When an interval or a unison begins to get out of tune, it will first develop waves, then beats.

CENTS

We have noted the division of musical sounds into tones and semi-tones, but there is still a more precise division used by the tuner. This is known as "cents" and further divides the semi-tone or half-tone into 100 parts or cents. A good way to remember this is to associate it with a dollar which is 100 cents. This is of course equal to 200 cents to a whole-tone. Think of a $2. bill.

After it is trained to do so, the human ear can detect pitch differences as little as 2 or 3 cents.

Cycles, Beats And Waves

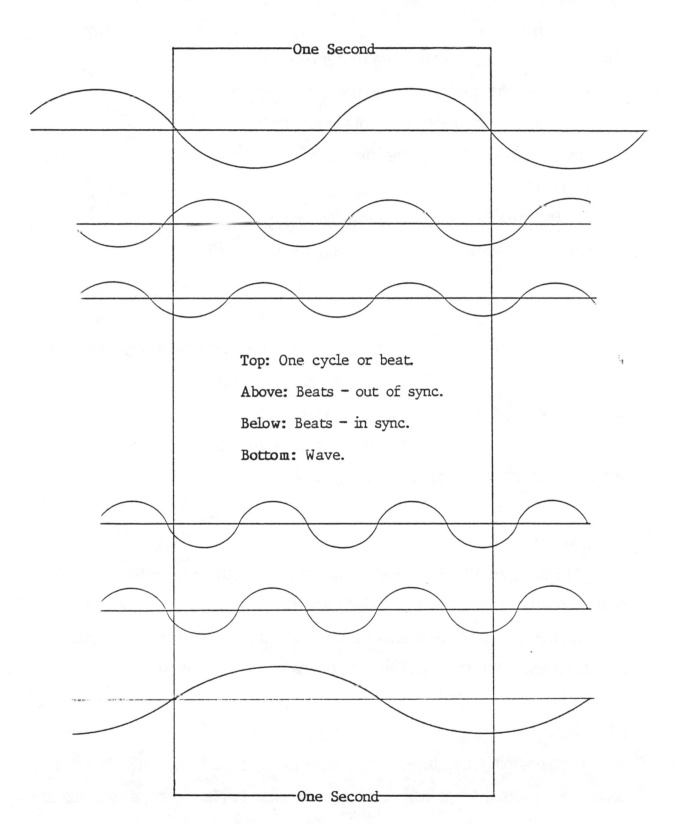

Top: One cycle or beat.

Above: Beats — out of sync.

Below: Beats — in sync.

Bottom: Wave.

TECHNIQUES

STRING SEGMENTS

The string is divided into five pressure segments:

1. From the tuning pin to the pressure bar, or agraffe.

2. From the pressure bar to the plate bridge.(short)

3. From the plate bridge to the first bridge pin. (This is the "speaking" section of the string).

4. From the first bridge pin to the second bridge pin.

5. From the second bridge pin to the hitch pin.

When the tension of the string is changed by tuning, this tension must be equally distributed throughout the five string segments in order to achieve a stable tuning. To do this the tuner strikes the key many times during the tuning of each string. This not only makes the condition of the string audible to the tuner, but helps equalize the change in tension throughout the five segments. If this is not done, sooner or later the tension will equalize itself and thus put the string out of tune again.

PLAYING THE KEYS

Do not pound the piano when tuning but strike the keys with authority; it is not possible to tune a piano quietly and properly. While changing the tuning lever to the next pin, begin striking the next note to be tuned. This activates the string and gives the tuner an idea of the string's condition.

PARTIALS

Another thing the tuner hears, consciously or unconsciously, is partials; sometimes referred to as harmonics or overtones. In piano strings, partials are caused by the string vibrating in divided segments within itself. The nodes, or segment points of the string that are the perimeters of the partials, cancel each other out to some degree; therefore, the partials with odd numbers (3rds, 5ths, 7ths, 9ths, etc.) are more easily heard. Partials apply to all strings and usually occur in an orderly sequence.

Partials, overtones and harmonics are the devices that create delicate nuiance in music and cause it to stir the emotions and touch the soul. The ability of a quality piano to produce well balanced partials is in sharp contrast to its smaller and inexpensive cousins.

Here are the fundamental and first 19 partials of C-2:

Fund....C-2	7th.....C-5	14th....B-5
1st.......C-3	8th....D-5	15th....C-6
2nd.......G-3	9th....E-5	16th....C#-6
3rd.......C-4	10th...F#-5	17th....D-6
4th.......E-4	11th...G-5	18th....D#-6
5th.......G-4	12th...A-5	19th....E-6
6th.......Bb-4	13th...A#-5	

A knowledge of partials will be useful later and will help explain why some strings are difficult to distinguish clearly.

DEMONSTRATION OF PARTIALS

Find a reasonably in-tune piano and during this demonstration do not use the sustaining pedal.

With the left hand, depress C-3 very slowly so the hammer does not touch the string or make any sound. While holding C-3 with the left hand, use the right hand to briskly strike a 3-note chord of G-4, C-5 and E-5, letting these keys up right away but still holding the C-3.

Listen carefully to the sound that remains and you will hear all four notes displayed in the partials of the C-3 strings.

PARTIALS

Fnd/ 1/ 2/ 3/ 4/ 5/ 6/ 7/ 8/ 9/ 10/ 11/ 12/ 13/ 14/ 15/ 16/ 17/ 18/ 19/

↑
Middle C

TUNING PRECAUTION

Make this an ironclad rule; NEVER move a string with the tuning lever that isn't vibrating and sounding. Unless the tuner can hear the string's sound, he has no way of knowing what is really happening with the tension. It could be possible the lever is on the wrong pin and pulling a string that is not sounding because it is muted — or there might be some obstacle impeding the string's vibrations. Continued pulling could cause string breakage and time consuming repair. If the sound of the string does not change when the tuning lever is moved, check to find the cause of the problem before continuing.

There will be an occasional piano where the string sound is slow to respond to the movement of the tuning lever. Make sure this is the case, and not faulty muting or lever placement, before breaking any strings.

SETTING THE TUNING PIN

After you have practiced tuning some unisons and octaves, begin forming the habit of "setting" the tuning pins. Just putting the strings in place without setting the tuning pins would lengthen the tuning process and greatly shorten the time the piano would stay in tune.

Form the habit of setting the pins as you are learning to tune as this will help determine your reputation as a good tuner.

When a string is pulled up, two minute things take place regarding the tuning pin. Due to the tension exerted on it, the pin develops a slight "twist". Also, the folicles of the wood surrounding the pin are moved in one direction. If the pin is not "set", in a very short time the pin will "un-twist" itself and the wood folicles will reverse, causing much of the tuner's work to be wasted.

As previously mentioned in "Lever Movements", after the string is put in the vicinity of where it is to be set, it is jockeyed into place with minute lever movements. Setting consists of putting the string 2 or 3 beats above its resting place, then, while still repeatedly striking that key, nudge the pin downward into place, letting the vibrations of the string assist in the setting process.

DIRECTIONS OF TUNING

Before getting into actual tuning, the student should be forming some idea of the overall tuning pattern.

After the temperament octave is set (F-3 to F-4), the tuner then tunes octaves to the right until he reaches the break at the end of the tenor section. He then proceeds left from the the temperament octave, completing the octave tuning in the tenor section in that direction. He continues on into the bass until the left end of the bass is reached, then removes the felt strip from the bass and, tuning every other pin, proceeds left again, completing the bass unisons. Next, he begins at the left end of the tenor section and tunes the tenor unisons, proceeding to the right until F#-4 is reached.

At this point he moves the lever to the left end of the treble section and tunes octaves to the right until he reaches the end of the treble section on C-8 (key #88). He then goes back to F#-4 and again proceeds in a right direction, tuning out the unisons in the remainder of the tenor section, going on into the treble section and tuning the unisons until key #88 is reached.

Usually, this procedure must be repeated a second time and then each unison is checked for any slippage. The foregoing description is to give the student an idea of tuning format. This routine has been found to be efficient and quick. Most tuners develop their own order of procedure after trying several, to see which suits them best.

TUNING PRACTICE
PRACTICE TIME

To learn to play an instrument well, it is necessary to devote some time every day to practice. This also applies to tuning. Set aside some time in the morning and afternoon or evening and begin by doing unisons and octaves for a half hour, twice a day. Do this for two weeks, then start practicing setting the temperament octave. Work at the temperament for at least two weeks before going on to the full piano. This foundation practice is essential and habits that are formed during this time will help or hinder you later – so try to be precise, patient and persistent.

Gradually increase your practice time to two, one-hour periods a day. To help your mind absorb what you are learning, do not practice one day a week.

This practice time is the dues everyone must pay to become a good tuner but, as the mind begins to grasp these new skills, the practice will become more easy and less tiring. Remember, the time spent in practice now will pay off later.

FIRST TUNING PRACTICE

Take the correct position at the piano, standing or sitting, depending on the type of piano you are using. Press Middle-C and watch the hammer so you can find the Middle-C unison strings. Place a rubber stick mute between the right Middle-C usison string and the next 3 unison strings to the right.

Place the tuning lever on the top tuning pin of the Middle-C unison. (This is the one for the left string.) Place the handle up, at the correct clock position. Look along the string and make sure it is on the correct pin, the left one of the 3 Middle-C unison strings.

Put your right hand on the lever in the second position. With the middle or index finger of your left hand, repeatedly play Middle C while moving the lever handle to the left. You should be able to hear the pitch go down as the string is lowered. Remember, always keep striking the key as you move the tuning lever. Lower the string only about 1/4 to 1/2 tone.

Now, slowly pull up the same string while striking the key again and listen to the beats get slower and slower until they stop. If you continue past the "perfect" point, you will notice the beats start up again. This law of beat generation applies, whether the string is sharp or flat. Do not pull the string very far past this perfect point, just enough so you can hear some beats pulsating. To continue to raise the string very far might cause the string to break. Repeat this exercise a few times to get used to the feel of the lever and the sound of the beats and as you listen to the beats, count them softly to yourself as they pulsate.

As you finish practicing on this string, leave it as close to the perfect point as you can, then place the mute on the other side of the unison and move the tuning lever to the bottom pin of this unison.(Look along the string to make sure of the right pin). Do the same thing you did with the first string, taking it slowly, down, then up a little past the perfect point, listening carefully to the sound of the beats. As you finish, leave this string as close to the perfect point as you can. You have just tuned your first unison.

Now go to F-4 (F above Middle-C and do the same procedure, inserting the mute to the right of the unison, moving the left string down, then up, then leaving it "in unison". Then insert the mute on the left and move the right string; down, then up and leave it in unison. Now rest.

Do this unison practice for a half hour at a time, twice a day for a few days, but do the half hour in short segments, stopping every few minutes to rest your ears. At the end of this time you should notice your ear is much more perceptive to identifying the beats.

UNISON PRACTICE

By now your ears should be accustomed to distinguishing beats so we will go on to serious unison practice. Tuning unisons is one of the major parts of tuning so the more proficient you become at it, the better your finished tuning job will be later on.

This time we will be tuning the unisons of the complete octave from Middle-C (C-4) to C-5, beginning with C-4 and going upward chromatically to C#-4, D-4, D#-4, etc. Do the same as you did before with the stick mute, putting it first to the right and tuning the left string, then to the left and tuning the right string. Unlike before, do not lower or raise the string unnecessarily, just pull it up or down to match the middle string of the unison. If you become confused, stop and rest a while. Try to get the strings as close to "matching" as you can. They may be a little ragged at first but your accuracy will improve with practice.

After you have gone through this octave of unisons once, refer to the section on Setting The Tuning Pin and begin doing this as you go along. This way, you will be developing two skills at the same time. Continue this unison practice for one week.

TUNING OCTAVES

Refer to the section "Using Strip Mutes" and mute the entire tenor section of the piano. Find the second last unison on the left of the tenor section, then find its octave <u>an octave higher</u> and place the tuning lever in the correct position on the <u>middle</u> tuning pin of that unison.

With your little finger and thumb of the left hand, play this octave, carefully watching the hammers and checking the strings to make sure the lever is on the correct pin. Play the octave and move the tuning pin, up or down a little, to match the sound. Of course the sound will be different from the unison practice in that the string you are tuning is an octave higher than the string your are tuning it to, but the pitch is comparative. It may help to strike the lower key and hold it, just before striking the upper key of the octave. This makes the sound comparisons more vivid and is also recommended procedure when tuning the upper treble and lower bass.

Try to move the tuning pin as little as possible to achieve your goal. Store this rule for permanent reference. It will save you time and trouble and make for a better tuning job.

Tune all the octaves in the tenor section, progressing to the right until you reach the last unison. Insert two stick mutes together by the right hand string of the last unison to mute it off, then tune that octave.

During this practice, take frequent breaks but be conscientious about getting in your practice time.

Combine this octave practice with the unison practice and do them from forty-five minutes to one hour, twice a day for two weeks. Remember to listen and count the beats as you set the strings in place.

SETTING THE TEMPERAMENT
EQUAL TEMPERAMENT

Equal temperament is a system of dividing the octave of 13 notes into 12 equal parts or intervals. Webster's dictionary defines equal temperament as "slightly modifying the pure scale".

If the temperament of a keyboard instrument was not "equal", music played on that instrument would sound acceptable in some keys and terrible in others, since the same type intervals would be of different widths in different keys. With equal temperament, intervals have the same value in all keys. For example; the distance from C to C# would be the same as from E to F or G# to A.

Equal temperament has been designed and proven, both scientifically and mathematically, and is the foundation of tuning. The ability to set a good temperament has much to do with determining the reputation of a tuner.

THE TEMPERAMENT OCTAVE

The temperament octave is the foundation for tuning the piano and all other notes on the piano are tuned in relation to it. It is located in the center of the keyboard, from the F below to the F above Middle C (from F-33 to F-45). Temperament is set in the middle of the piano because beats are more easily heard there than in higher or lower areas.

THE TEMPERAMENT INTERVALS

Unlike tuning unisons and octaves, where the tuner strives to tune the strings as close to "perfect" or beatless as possible, the temperament intervals are deliberately tuned imperfect so they will be spaced equally. To achieve this, the fourths are expanded and the fifths are contracted.

Following is a list of steps for setting the temperament octave. Remember, # means sharp and b means flat.

Normally, if the pitch is not too low, the first step in tuning is to tune C-4 to the C tuning fork. For the present, however, omit this step.

TEMPERAMENT TUNING STEPS

STEP 1.

Tune target note	F–4
Slightly (#,b,or beatless)	#
To source note	C–4
[Reference note]	F–5
To check, compare intervals	None
Second interval should beat	——

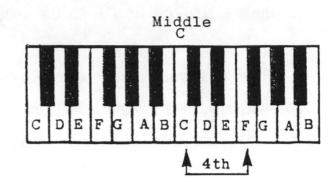

STEP 2.

Tune target note	F–3
Slightly (#,b,or beatless)	Beatless
To source note	F–4
[Reference note]	None
To check, compare intervals to C#–3 & F–4	C#–3 & F–3
Second interval should beat	Same speed

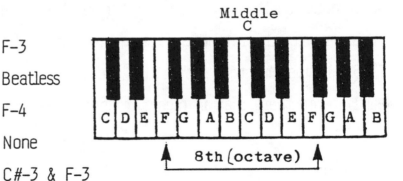

STEP 3.

Tune target note	A#–3
Slightly (#,b,or beatless)	#
To source note	F–3 or F–4
[Reference note]	A#–4
To check, compare intervals	None
Second interval should beat	——

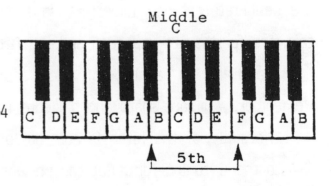

STEP 4.

Tune target note	G-3
Slightly (#,b,or beatless)	b
To source note	C-4
[Reference note]	G-4
To check, compare intervals	None
Second interval should beat	——

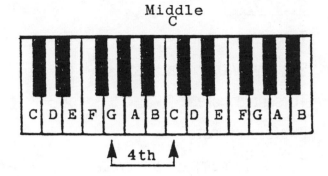

STEP 5.

Tune target note	D-4
Slightly (#,b,or beatless)	b
To source note	G-3
[Reference note]	D-5
To check, compare intervals to A#-3 & D-4	G-3 & A#-3
Second interval should beat	Slower

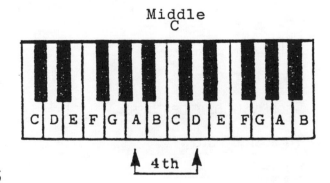

STEP 6.

Tune target note	A-3
Slightly (#,b,or beatless)	b
To source note	D-4
[Reference note]	A-4
To check, compare intervals to F-3 & D-4	F-3 & A-3
Second interval should beat	Faster

STEP 7.

Tune target note	E-4
Slightly (#,b,or beatless)	b
To source note	A-3
[Reference note]	E-5
To check, compare intervals to G-3 & E-4	F-3 & D-4
Second interval should beat	Faster

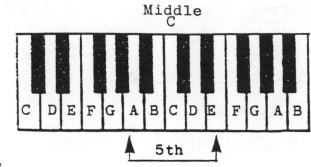

STEP 8.

Tune target note	B-3
Slightly (#,b,or beatless)	b
To source note	E-4
[Reference note]	B-4
To check, compare intervals to F-3 & D-4	G-3 & B-3
Second interval should beat	Same speed

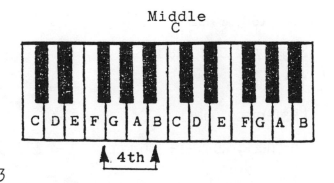

STEP 9.

Tune target note	F#-3
Slightly (#,b,or beatless)	b
To source note	B-3
[Reference note]	F#-4
To check, compare intervals to F#-3 & A#-3	F-3 & A-3
Second interval should beat	Faster

STEP 10.

Tune target note	C#-4
Slightly (#,b,or beatless)	b
To source note	F#-3
[Reference note]	C#-5
To check, compare intervals	F#-3 & A#-3
to F#-3 & C#-3	
Second interval should beat	Faster

Middle C

STEP 11.

Tune target note	G#-3
Slightly (#,b,or beatless)	b
To source note	C#-4
[Reference note]	G#-4
To check, compare intervals	G-3 & B-3
to G#-3 & C-4	
Second interval should beat	Faster

Middle C

STEP 12.

Tune target note	D#-4
Slightly (#,b,or beatless)	b
To source note	G#-3
[Reference note]	D#-5
To check, compare intervals	G-3 & D-4
to G#-3 & D#-4	
Second interval should beat	Faster

Middle C

—At this point, D#-4 should be slightly flat of A#-3.

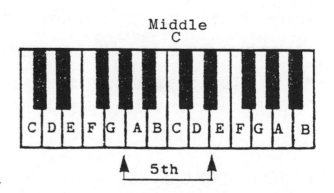

TUNING PROCEDURES

MAKING WAVES

In tuning the temperament intervals indicated in the Temperament Tuning Steps, the degree of contraction and expansion to be put into the intervals is quite small; actually, not even a beat but rather a wave; a part of a beat.

When the temperament cycle is completed there should be no beats in the intervals, but don't worry if it takes you much practice to get this to happen; this is normal. It will come, along with endurance, strength and speed, as your ear grows stronger and more accute and your muscles become attuned to minute control.

TUNE FORWARD AND BACKWARD

If there are beats in the last interval of the temperament (D#-4 & A#-3), begin at the end and work backward. That is, start with making F-4 a wave sharp of C-4, then F-4 (again) sharp of A#-3, then D#-4 a little sharp of G#-3, etc. and continue backward, making all the intervals, first 4ths then 5ths, all a little sharp as you go back through the cycle until you reach G-3 which is tuned a wave flat of C-4.

In order to get the temperament octave even, this procedure of going up and back and up and back can be done until the spare beats are pushed out.

This up and back routine makes temperament tuning easier and saves time.

TESTS AND CHECKS

To speed up the detection of uneveness and flaws in the temperament octave, several tests may be run.

RUNNING THIRDS

One of the most useful tests is the running of 3rds up the entire temperament octave. If the intervals are spaced correctly, the beats in the 3rds will gradually and evenly increase in speed as they progress up the scale. Play each two notes together and move fairly rapidly up the scale so the speed of the beats can be compared easily. Here is a list:

F-3 & A-3

F#-3 & A#-3

G-3 & B-3

G#-3 & C-4

A-3 & C#-4

A#-3 & D-4

B-3 & D#-4

C-4 & E-4

C#-4 & F-4

RUNNING SIXTHS

Here is another similar check. The 6ths also should gradually increase in speed as they are run up the scale.

F-3 & D-4

F#-3 & D#-4

G-3 & E-4

G#-3 & F-4

RUNNING FOURTHS

Since there should be no beats in the temperament fourths, this test will act as a beat detector.

F-3 & A#-3

F#-3 & B-3

G-3 & C-3

G#-3 & C#-3

A-3 & D-3

A#-3 & D#-3

RUNNING FIFTHS

Fifths also should be beatless. This is another beat detector.

F-3 & C-4

F#-3 & C#-4

G-3 & D-4

G#-3 & D#-4

A-3 & E-4

A#-3 & F-4

CHECKS FOR CLEANER FIFTHS

The wave tolerance in 5ths is less than it is in 4ths. That is, if there must be slight discrepancy in the temperament intervals, this "slack" should be in the 4ths, not the 5ths, which should be as clean as possible.

After the temperament octave has been gone over and there is a semblance of order to the intervals, tune F#-4 to F#-3. This additional note (F#-4) is necessary to running these 5ths checks. Play these 4-way chords and listen for clarity. If they don't have it, the 5ths are not spaced correctly.

(These are major 7th chords; abbreviated: maj.7th).

F-3, A-3, C-4, E-4

F#-3,A#-3,C#-4,F-4

G-3, B-3, D,4, F#-4

EXPANDING ERRORS

Errors that are left in the temperament octave are used as references for tuning the rest of the piano. When this is done, a peculiar situation occurs: As the tuning is expanded to the right and to the left, these errors are gradually magnified as the tuning progresses further away from the temperament. What may seem like a minor roughness in the temperament octave gradually grows into harshness as the tuning spreads. If you keep this in mind, you will be less inclined to leave beats in the temperament octave.

REPAIRING THE TEMPERAMENT INTERVALS

After you become more familiar with the temperament and running the checks, you can determine quickly which intervals need adjusting and in which direction.

For example; when running the 3rds, if the G#-3, C-4 3rd beats too slow, this would indicate the G#-3 is too sharp.

With practice, this will all become familiar to you and needed adjustments can be quickly identified and repaired.

TEMPERAMENT PRACTICE

Insert the strip mute in the tenor section and any of the bass section that may be within a 3rd of the temperament, following the instructions in the

"Using The Mutes" section. Use the temperament keyboard diagrams and begin setting the temperament octave. Don' worry if it is rough at first; accuracy and speed will come.

Do a half-hour to forty-five minutes work with the temperament twice a day. Also, continue doing the unison and octave practice for fifteen minutes, twice a day. Do this for two weeks before going on to the full piano.

TUNING THE FULL PIANO

Some of this has been touched upon in previous sections but we will go over the procedure here in it's entirety and proper order.

1. Strip mute the entire piano.

2. Decide on the pitch. (This will be covered in a later section.)

3. Set the temperament octave.

4. Tune the tenor section octaves to the right until you reach the end of the section.

5. Tune the tenor octaves to the left till you reach the end of the section.

6. Tune the bass octaves, proceeding left. Remember, tune every other un-muted string in the two-string area.

7. Remove the strip mute from the bass section and tune the previously muted strings by tuning every other string, then go on leftward through the single strings to the bottom (A-0). More on this later.

8. Begin tuning the unisons in the tenor section, starting at the left side. Tune the left string, remove the strip mute loop from the right side of the unison, insert a stick mute by the left string and tune the right string. Proceed rightward in this fashion until you reach F#-4, then stop.

9. Tune the treble octaves rightward to the end (C-88). More on this later.

10. Go back to the tenor section and moving to the right, finish tuning out the tenor unisons.

11v. **For verticals,** carefully pull the strip mute from behind the treble dampers and the rest of the treble section. Using a stick mute, first on the right side, then moving it to the left side of the unison, tune out the treble unisons, proceeding rightward to the end (C-88).

11g. **For grands,** do not remove the strip mute from the treble as with the verticals. Proceed rightward, removing one loop at a time and using the stick mute as described in step 8.

TUNING REFINEMENTS
OCTAVE CHECK

Test the purity of an octave with a major 6th and a minor 3rd. If the octave is pure, they should beat the same. Example: To check D-3 & D-4, play D-3 & F-3, then F-3 & D-4. Compare the beats. This may be used to check any octave where the beats can be distinguished.

THE UPPER TREBLE

As you proceed into the higher frequencies, the pitch becomes a little more difficult to distinguish. To aid in this situation, use broken octaves. That is, instead of playing both notes of the octave at the same time, play the bottom (left) note first and hold it, just before striking the top note of the octave.

Another help in this area is to play lower single notes of that key on up to the one you are tuning. For example, if you are tuning G-7, play in this order: G-4. G-5, G-6, and then G-7. This will give you more of a reference in the high notes.

STRETCH TUNING

If the treble octaves of a piano were tuned beatless all the way to the top (C-88), most people would say the treble was flat. Because of this strange nature of the human ear, we employ what is known as "stretch" tuning, or the gradual widening of the octaves as they progress toward the top end of the piano. This must be done with great subtlety and with gradually increasing degrees of a few cents each at each increase point. This is another item for particular attention and an electronic tuning aid can be of great help here. (See section on Electronic Tuning, page 125.)

The following is a list of suggested cents increases for stretch tuning, and where they occur. All cents given are from zero and not added to each other.

F#-5   3cts.#

C-6   6cts.#

F#-6   9cts.#

C-7   12cts.#

F#-7   15cts.#

C-8   18cts.#

In contrast, the bass gradually gets _flatter_ in about the same degrees.

THE LOWER BASS

Some lower bass notes are difficult to distinguish, especially on the smaller and cheaper pianos which have a high degree of inharmonicity in the bass strings. Here again, playing the octave notes one at a time is a great help, but in the bass, reverse the order and play the top (right) note first and hold it, then strike the bottom note. Listen for the <u>bottom</u> of the sound.

Another help in checking the bass is the running of 10ths to the left. Example: Begin with the 10th of C-2, E-3 and progress down to B-1, D#-3, then A#-1, D-3, etc.

There will be times when these devices are of little help and it will be up to the tuner's ear to determine the setting of the lower bass strings. Don't labor over an obscure situation. Use your best judgement and go on.

PITCH DECISION

Before tuning a piano, a practical decision must be made as to what pitch it should be set. Many "experts" advocate tuning all pianos to A-440. This is extremely impractical and could heap much difficulty on the aspiring tuner.

1st. Determine the present pitch of the instrument by checking it with the C-523.3 tuning fork.

2nd. Estimate the age of the piano. If over 30 years old, it is suspect.

3rd. Find out what the piano will be used for and if it will be played with other musical instruments.

4th. With the tuning lever and a stick mute, test a few tuning pins at random to determine if the piano will hold a tuning well and/or sustain a pitch raise.

5th. Inquire as to when the piano was tuned last.

With the above information, make a decision as to which pitch to tune the piano. For example; If the piano is reasonably new (2 to 5 years) and is only slightly below A-440, it would certainly be proper to tune it a A-440.

However, if the piano is old, let's say 60 years, and is a half tone flat of A-440, and is going to be played by itself, raising the pitch would be unnecessary and impractical. To attempt to do so could result in string breakage and would require much extra time to stabilize the necessary multiple tunings, which might not hold for long.

After some experience and talking to piano owners, you will develop the ability of deciding on the best course of action. A general rule of thunmb is: If the pitch is very far below A-440 and it isn't absolutely necessary that it be raised, don't raise it. But before tuning, let the customer know your decision and explain why you arrived at it.

RAISING THE PITCH

The reasons for and against raising the pitch of a piano were discussed in the foregoing section. Should it be absolutely necessary to do so and the piano and strings are in a condition to tolerate the added strain, this section will explain the procedure. Keep in mind that raising the pitch 1/2 tone adds over two tons of tension to the instrument.

If a piano is over a whole tone flat of A-440, do not attempt to raise it all the way unless you are sure it will take the strain. If you decide to do so, raise it a half tone at a time and rough-tune the complete piano at this level before going on to raise the pitch the remainder of the way. Of course there will be some slippage. It is estimated that in pitch raising, the pitch may slip back as much as one third.

Of course, in pitch raising, the tuning will need to be gone over several times until it is stabilized. This can usually be done in one session (the same day) but allow enough time for the extra work. Usually, pitch raising over 1/4 tone involves extra charges, so advise the customer accordingly before beginning the work. Some tuners have a set fee for each quarter tone raised.

LOWERING PITCH

Lowering the pitch by any significant amount is rare. If it is absolutely necessary, the same general procedures apply, only in reverse, as raising pitch.

FINE TUNING

Fine tuning is simply more precise tuning or "polishing". The way to achieve it is to go over the whole tuning process a second, and sometimes even a third time. Each time you will notice differences in some of the notes, due to the pitch dropping slightly or simply a slight variance with your first tuning.

This second (and third) tuning is done at the same sitting, however, it does not take as long as the first.

After you have gone over the piano two (or three) times, check the unisons and octaves to see if any strings have slipped out a little and are causing waves or even beats. There are usually a few. Use the lever and stick mutes to clean them up: With the strip mutes out of the piano, play all the keys and listen for waves or beats. If you hear some, place a stick mute first on one side, then the other and try to determine which string is out. If the center string is causing the problem, mute off the side strings with the stick mutes and re-tune that octave, also checking the following octaves of that note on to the end. This sounds laborious but it only takes a few additional minutes to check out the piano and makes for a neater job.

ELECTRONIC TUNING

Though the market abounds with many types of electronic tuners, using one for piano tuning is still controversial. Much of the negative attitude in this area was probably brought about by tuners using these devices to set the temperament octave, which leaves much to be desired. Here, instead of tuning one note to another, notes are tuned to the machine, thus leaving a much wider margin for error.

As for types, there are electronic tuners with tone emission to match, rotating wheels that indicate pitch change, rotating lights, fluctuating needles in frequency meters, etc., etc.

The most practical of these devices are the ones with the rotating lights, many of which are used in piano factories. The red lights rotate in response to frequencies near the pitch that is selected on a dial and rotate to the right when the sound is sharp, to the left when it is flat, and stop when the sound is precisely on pitch. These tuners can be calibrated to any pitch, thus enabling their use with old pianos where the pitch cannot be brought near A-440.

One of the best and most useful of this type tuner is the Hale "Sight-O-Tuner", available from Hale Piano Supply Company. The best use of this tuner is in "stretching" in the upper treble and in the lower bass where tones are obscure.

Also, if a piano technician develops a hearing problem concerning the higher pitches, one of these devices could add years to his working life,

Used with astute moderation, these devices can be a good thing. The biggest mistake concerning them is to attempt to substitute the machine for tuning ability. It simply won't work. To put it another way; An electronic tuning device will enhance the work of a good tuner but it will not make a good tuner out of a bad one. A good electronic tuner similar to the Sight-O-Tuner is expensive but in the long run is worth it. It saves time and frustration and can add that extra polish to a good tuning job.

TUNING DURABILITY

Tuning durability depends on several factors, some of which are quite variable.

1: Temperature and hunmidity change.

2: Age and condition of the piano.

3: Location of the piano.

4: Abuse of the instrument, if any.

5: What use the piano will be put to.

6: Tuning quality and thoroughness.

The general opinion is that a piano should be tuned every six months. At the outside, at <u>least</u> once a year. If the piano is very new, it will need more frequent tunings to get the strings and tension "settled in". Large or heavy pianos hold a tuning better than small or light ones. Pianos in small churches, where the temperature and humidity fluctuate extremely, need more frequent tunings. Clumsy and pounding players are bad for a tuning job and the piano in general. Little children that beat on the keys can wreck a tuning.

Pianos should never be placed by a window, in the direct sunlight, near a heater or vent or near an outside door that is used frequently. Air conditioning can sometimes make some sections grow sharp. Also, large nearby bodies of water can cause a tuning job to be of short duration.

Another consideration is its use. Some night club players have their pianos tuned every few weeks, while concert artists have theirs tuned before each performance.

Once the customers circumstances and needs have been determined, a suitable tuning schedule can be set up to meet these individual requirements.

....

Section 5. Other Piano Items

Above: Piano Dolly

PIANO MOVING

A piano is a precision instrument, not just a piece of furniture and when it is moved it should be handled with great care. Depending on its size, a piano can weigh from 300 to 2000 pounds.

The use of a piano dolly and accessories is almost a necessity in most cases and in some situations, it is an absolute necessity in order to control the weight of the unwieldy instrument. These can usually be rented for a small fee from a music store that handles pianos. The accessories consist of several mover's blankets and two or three long, heavy straps for securing the piano to the dolly. These dollies have a tall padded end with metal handles that unfold to aid in moving and lifting. The other end of the dolly has two heavy strap handles for the same purpose.

For the smaller pianos, a minimum of 2 persons is required if one of them has had some previous experience. For the larger pianos, a minimum of three. If experienced help is not available, add one or two men to the moving job. Also add men if there are stairs involved. Be sure to measure any tight areas the piano may have to go through <u>before</u> the moving job. It will save much trouble and time.

After the piano is placed on the dolly, it should be wrapped in blankets and strapped securely to the dolly. This protects the piano's finish when rounding corners and going through doorways, etc.

VERTICALS

Nearly all verticals have wooden handles between the posts on each side of the back. If the piano is small, a person can grasp one of these handles in one hand and under the keyboard with the other hand. With another person doing this same thing at the other end, the piano may be lifted on and off the dolly. Make certain the casters are not riding on the dolly rails.

GRANDS

Moving a grand piano is somewhat more complicated and unless the movers have had experience with moving grands, it would be wise to have the job done by professional movers.

In order to move a grand piano, it must first be partially disassembled. To assist in this operation, a small, padded saw horse, slightly higher than the bottom of the keybed is needed.

First, remove the pedals and pedal lyre, which is detached as a unit by taking out some screws from the top beam of the lyre into the bottom of the piano. Also remove the lyre braces.

Facing the keyboard of the piano, lift the left front leg and push the padded saw horse under the case near the leg. Remove any bolts or screws that are holding the leg and push the leg toward the center of the piano to disengage the leg plate. Remove the leg and lay it aside.

Move the piano dolly along the left side of the piano and position it with the high part in front. Now, lift the left front corner of the piano and remove the saw horse. Lower the left front of the piano until the corner rests on the felt pad near the front of the dolly. Make sure the lip of the lid fits over the edge of the dolly risers so it is not damaged. Some movers remove the piano lid during moving. Have one person steady the piano as it is raised on its flat side onto the dolly.

Remove the other two legs, wrap the piano with the blankets and strap it down. With grands, the straps are placed around the tall end and in the curve, then a very long third strap is tied around the tops of these and secured at the tall end of the dolly.

To set up the piano again, go through the same procedure in reverse.

Again, a note of caution: If the job looks too tough or complicated, call in professional piano movers. Let them take the risk — they're insured. Don't take unnecessary chances, especially with someone else's property. Then too, when the inexperienced attempt to move heavy painos, there is always the possibility of personal injury to consider.

MOVING PIANOS AROUND A ROOM

Contrary to popular belief, an accasional moving of a piano to a different part of the room will not cause it to go out of tune, unless the new location itself contains elements that would cause this to happen.

However, when moving pianos without benefit of a dolly, there are some very definite no-nos. <u>Never</u> push a grand piano on a carpet! This can cause leg breakage, even on new pianos and especially on old ones. Get three or four sturdy persons and "Lift" it as it is moved, thus taking the strain off the legs.

When moving verticals with front legs, slightly tilt the piano back, so as to take the weight off the legs, especially on a carpet.

REPLACING SETS OF KEY TOPS

Replacing of individual key tops has been covered in a previous section. To replace an entire set of key tops, the keys should be removed from the piano and taken to the shop. Make sure they are numbered or marked by drawing a diagonal line from just behind the capstan of key 1 to just behind the key top of key 88. Another sorting time saver is to remove the keys 10 or 12 at a time and re-assemble them in order on a flat surface, then wrap them in this position, near the center, using wide masking tape.

In the shop, lay the keys out on the work bench or a flat surface and keep them in order during the re-topping process.

Remove the old key tops by standing each key on its end on a firm surface and wedging the knife blade between the key wood and the keytop and pushing downward. If the knife digs into the grain of the key wood and begins to split it, turn the key on the other end and repeat the same procedure.

Individual heads and tails <u>can</u> be used for topping entire sets; however, using pre-formed one-piece keytops makes a more professional-looking job. These molded plastic tops are available in sets with the heads and tails in one piece and also with the heads, tails and fronts in one piece. (The front is the square thin white lamination on the front of the key).

To accommodate the wide variety of key sizes, these molded tops are slightly oversized. Using piano key cement, the key tops are applied and allowed to dry overnight. The excess edges must then be trimmed and sanded. To do this properly and quickly, the use of some machinery is necessary.

TOPPING MACHINERY

There is professional keytopping machinery available but it is expensive and unless the technician intends to do a high volume of keytopping business, purchasing this epecialized machinery is not practical.

For the edge-trimming operation, an edge trimmer, mounted in a radial arm saw, a drill press or a router may be used, providing the speed is over 3000 RPM. For cleaning up the corners and rough edges, a small belt sander is ideal. This later job may be attempted with a hand file but this is extremely tedious.

These small machine tools have many other uses and are comparatively inexpensive. They will pay for themselves in just a few key-topping jobs.

After the keys have been topped, edged and the corners, etc. carefully cleaned up with the sander, inspect each key and clean up any rough spots with a hand file, and the job is done.

New plastic sharps are installed in the same way; however, these require no edging or sanding operation, just glue them on.

HAVING THE KEYS RE-TOPPED

The larger piano supply houses do topping jobs at a reasonable cost but this involves shipping the keys to them and waiting for their return. This additional time and charges may cause a customer to shy away from having the job done — but this is an alternative to doing it yourself.

YOUR OWN KEY TOPPING BUSINESS

Some technicians go into key topping as a sideline business. If there is no such business in your area, it might be worth your while to look into this. In any event, having the facilities to do your own key topping is profitable, even on a small scale.

REBUILDING PIANOS

The rebuilding, refurbishing or restoring of pianos is a rewarding undertaking, both in money and satisfaction. It is suggested, however, that the novice technician aquire some general experience before undertaking any rebuilding jobs and inexperienced persons should only attempt this with their own pianos.

Rebuilding, etc. means different things to different people. In general, it involves the installation of new underfelts, new strings and tuning pins, sometimes new hammers or even all the action units, new key tops, complete regulation to the action and quite often refinishing.

Before taking on a job of this magnitude, the piano should be carefully checked to see what work needs to be done. Determine the age of the piano by looking up the serial number in the Pierce Piano Atlas. See if there is any serious structural damage that would prevent the piano from having a good sound after the work is completed. After all necessary information has been assembled, determine if the piano is worth restoring and estimate your cost in time and parts and determine what you intend to charge for the job. Present this information to the customer, along with the estimated time it will take to complete the job. These extensive jobs are always done best in the shop, if you have access to one, and this would also involve the cost of moving the piano to and from the shop.

Most old pianos, especially the smaller verticals, are simply not worth rebuilding, so this type of work is usually confined to the better old grands. Of course, there are degrees in between and it is up to the technicann and the piano owner to what extent and expense this work should go,

The individual operations involved in rebuilding pianos are covered in the various sections of this book.

RESTRINGING

The detailed procedure for the installation of individual strings is covered in the section on repair. This section will deal with the complete restringing job. Of course, the action should first be removed from the piano.

REMOVING THE OLD STRINGS

After the decision to restring the piano has been made and the instrument has been moved to the shop, proceed in the following order: Loosen and remove the bottom tuning pin (the one nearest the keyboard) of each unison, beginning at the first unwound string in the tenor section and continuing rightward through the top of the treble and key 88.

Measure two or three of these removed tuning pins with the tuning pin gauge (they should be the same size).

Select tuning pins of the same length but the next size _larger_ and place one of these in each of the holes where you have removed the old pins. Do not drive them in, just tap lightly, enough so they won't come out by accident. These are your marker pins to indicate where you should change wire sizes when restringing. If you have no tuning pins to use as markers, mark these holes with a piece of masking tape, or insert pencils.

Next, measure each loosened string with the piano wire gauge and carefully note its size and position in the configuration of tuning pins on a piece of paper.

Now, loosen all the strings, beginning in the low bass and working rightward, but do not loosen them chromatically. Loosen the bottom string, count 12 unisons and loosn another unison, count 12 and loosed another till you reach the end of the treble section. Now go back to the bottom and loosen the string next to the already loosened one and go on rightward, loosening the entire unison to the right of the already loosened strings. Keep this up until all the strings are loosened. Give each string at least one full turn to the left with the tuning lever or T handle. This system of loosening is necessary so the pressure of the strings will be reduced gradually and not put undue strain on any one section of the piano.

Use a piece of heavy wire and make a loop in one end about the size of a coin and wrap the wire end securely to mantain the loop. Remove the bass strings and old tuning pins from the bottom bass, one at a time, and put their hitch pin loops over the wire holder you just made. Remove all the wound strings and store them in order on the wire holder. These are to be sent to the string maker at a piano supply company for duplication. With the old set of strings, also include the name, serial number and any other information about the piano that the string maker may need for his duplicating job.

Next, remove the tenor and treble strings and tuning pins, taking care not to remove the new tuning pins you have used to mark the string size changes. NOTE: When removing the unwound strings, take note of any single strings with hitch pin loops and mark them on your chart.

MATERIALS

Measure the tuning pin's diameter and length and mark this information in your notes. You will need to order a set that is the same length but one size larger. (If 2/0, order 3/0, etc.) Determine from your notes what sizes and how much piano wire you will need. A piano technician should keep on hand some piano wire in various sizes. Ordering one pound coils of piano wire in all the 1/2 sizes from 13 to 20 is not extravagant as what is not used for the restringing job at hand will be used for other work, sooner or later.

Also, measure and order new hitch pin punchings and understring felts, the same sizes as the old ones.

Send off the order for these materials and any other items you will require in the rebuilding of the piano. Wrap the old bass strings in a coil of about 15 inches and tie them securely so they will not spring loose in shipment. Send these, along with the necessary information to the piano supply company and string maker.

WHILE THE STRINGS ARE OUT

With the strings out of the piano, now is the ideal time to thoroughly clean the soundboard and repair any large cracks with soundboard shims.

Run some yellow glue in the small cracks and wipe off the excess with a damp cloth. Scrape out the large cracks with a shimming tool and run some yellow glue in the cracks. Cut off the wood shim to the proper length and tap the thin edge into the crack and let dry overnight.

With a wood chisel, carefully cut off the excess shim level with the soundboard. With the appropriate stain and finish, touch up the shim edges to match the color of the soundboard.

After the shim touch-up work is dry, use old newspapers and masking tape to cover the soundboard, case, and anything else around and under the plate that may be exposed.

Check the plate screws/bolts to make sure they are tight.

Clean the plate with a cloth moistened with lacquer thinner, then spray-paint the plate, using a can of the appropriate gold-bronze color. Get everything under the strings looking as nice as possible before beginning to restring the piano.

INSTALLING THE NEW STRINGS

Install the necessary understring felts, including the small red felt hitch pin washers.

Re-check your marker pins and make sure you have the same string sizes on the same unisons. Remember, one wire is two strings. Also, on all tuning pins, the string must be wound clockwise, facing the square end of the pin. If you are restringing a grand, install a pin block jack.

Begin stringing at the upper treble with the smaller sizes of wire. Select the correct wire size. Pull out wire to the length needed and cut. Insert wire through hole in tuning pin and bend a 1/8 inch becket. Insert tuning pin in coil setter tool and turn two coils with the T handle. Place this pin in the correct hole and tap with the T handle. Run wire under frame brace or capo bar, or through the proper hole in any agraffes that may be present, then down around the proper hitch pin, and back via the same route, under capo bar or frame brace, etc. Run wire by the hole its next tuning pin will go in and measure four fingers past it and cut it off there. Insert in a tuning pin as before and tap it in its hole. Position the wire around the two sets of bridge pins, using the old grooves as guides.

Use hammer and a tuning pin punch and drive in the two tuning pins part way. Now, with the T handle on the tuning pin and a coil lifter under the coil, pull up the coil as you tighten each pin, making a nice close coil on each. Finish driving the pins in, but not too far. Leave 3/8 inch between the bottom of the coil and the plate. Go on to the next unit and repeat the operation.

Proceed to the unison with the marker pin and change to the next size wire indicated in your notes. Keep on, changing wire sizes at each marked unison, until you have reached the lower tenor.

The new bass strings go on last. Be sure to keep them in order as you go from right to left.

When you have finished installing all the strings, go over them and check the coils for uniformity and the evenness of the tops of the tuning pins. It may be necessary to tap a few in a little. Don't overdo this but try to make a neat appearing job and see that the strings are pulled tight – but not tight enough to break.

ALIGNING THE NEW STRINGS

Put the action back in the piano. Now the strings must be aligned to the hammers. If the piano has agraffes, this is already taken care of. If it does not, begin at key 88 and press the key and see that the hammer makes contact with all three strings. If it does not, use a screwdriver and/or the string spacer to move and space the strings until they are in line with the hammers. This is essential before tuning the strings.

TUNING THE NEW STRINGS

Insert the strip mutes throughout the sections of the piano, just like a regular tuning. Use the tuning fork to tune middle C and tune the Cs up and down, remembering that each has an octave difference to the last, going away from middle C. When in doubt, stop and rest. Do not pull a string to the point of breaking.

After you have the Cs, go to the C#s and do all those, then the Ds, etc. until you have gone through all the notes. Of course, this will be a very crude tuning. That doesn't matter. It won't hold well at first anyway. After you have gone through all the notes, begin removing the felt strip a loop at a time and tuning the side strings. Don't bother about precision, just get the string close to its intended sound.

It may be necessary to do this two or three times before the strings begin to sound anything like the are intended. Wait a few hours, or overnight between tunings to allow the new strings to stretch out.

After the sound of the strings is stabilized, apply three or four tunings, one each day or two. This should put the new strings in good shape. After the piano is moved back to the customer, it should be tuned again, plus every three months for two tunings, then it should be stabilized enough to hold a tuning for six months.

b # b # b # b # b # b

REFINISHING

REMOVING THE OLD FINISH

Refinishing a piano is a messy job and should be done in a suitable place, preferably a shop or a garage with a concrete floor. This job will take several days or weeks, during which time the piano cannot be used.

Determine first if the piano is worth the hours of work and the expense needed to do the job properly.

Inspect the case to see if there are many nicks, holes, gouges or broken corners that must be repaired.

Next, take the piano case apart: Take off the lid, the front, the fall board, the key stop rail, key blocks, key slip, and bottom board. Take apart any of these units that are contain multiple parts, such as the fall board assembly and music desk or rack. With grands, take off the pedal lyre and braces. It isn't necessary to remove the action and keys but cover them well to avoid damage from the refinishing materials.

Take off any hardware such as: lid hinges, music desk hinges, brackets, knobs, etc.

Put down plenty of old newspapers to absorb the dirty water from the refinishing. Use a good quality water–soluble, _thick_ paint and varnish remover and apply according to the directions. When it has done its work (usually about 15 or 20 minutes), scrape off the old gunk with a putty knife. It may be necessary to repeat this operation two or three times. After you have scraped as much as you can, clean the surface with medium steel wool, dipped in warm water. Let dry. If there are still some remaining spots, clean with steel wool dipped in the finish remover.

When removing the finish from the inside of the case of grands, be sure to mask off the plate and strings and use plenty of newspapers. It is a good idea not to use the water-soluble finish remover here as the cleaning water may damage the soundboard. Instead, use a self-containing liquid remover such as Homer Formby's and apply with fine steel wool. This requires more work but there is less chance of damaging the piano. Of course, the outside of the case and the other case parts may be stripped in the usual way.

While you are at it, remove the finish from part of the <u>inside</u> of the bottom board, or on grands, the fall board. This area can be used later to test different finishes and won't show on your finished job.

PREPARING THE WOOD

After you have removed the old finish from all of the parts, lightly sand the exposed surface with a medium fine sandpaper. Use a "matching" shade of a good wood filler such as Plastic Wood or Wood Dough, and fill any holes or damaged areas of the case. Allow for shrinkage.

After the wood filler had dried overnight, use a wood rasp to level and shape these repaired areas, then sand.

Put on some wood filler and sealer to close the pores in the newly exposed wood. Let dry and sand.

APPLYING THE NEW FINISH

Select the color of stain you intend to use. If the wood surface looks good, you may decide on a clear gloss or satin polyurethane finish which will darken the wood a shade or two. There are many ways to refinish a piano after the surface has been stripped. Use the test finish area to try a few.

Apply your selected finish to the piano and parts and let dry. Lightly sand with fine sand paper and fine steel wool and wipe with a clean cloth. If you are using stain, one coat may be quite sufficient but you will also need to apply a coat of clear polyurethane to protect the finish. Let dry and sand and rub with steel wool. If you are using a clear finish, apply a second coat and sand again.

Mix some stain with the clear finish and touch up the repaired spots to match their surrounding areas. Let dry and sand.

Apply a coat of good paste wax and hand rub.

FINISHING TOUCHES

Polish the brass hardware or replace it with new hardware from the piano supply catalogs. Put new felt on the key stop rail and other places that show. Replace the old rubber nails and buttons with new ones and reassemble the piano.

FINISHING COMMENTS

It is better to have some refinishing experience before taking on such a job for a customer. Even with experience, these jobs can be a little tricky in that exact shades of finish on the final product are not always predictable.

If the case of a piano is in too bad a condition to strip down and refinish, an alternative is to paint it with satin or semi-gloss black.

Whatever you decide to do with the finish, allow plenty of time to do the job correctly.

b # b # b # b # b # b

READING MUSIC

Though the ability to read music is not essential to tuning, it is a related skill and some knowledge of it should be acquired. This section contains only the very basics of music reading; excerpts from a more comprehensive coverage in another book by this author: "How To Read And Write Music Including Professional Chord Symbol Methed", available from this publisher.

THE STAFF

The staff is composed of five parallel lines and four spaces. It is the basis of all modern music writing. When the notes go up on the staff, they go up in pitch — down on the staff, down in pitch.

CLEFS

The clef sign is placed at the beginning of the staff to indicate a specific pitch. Here we will only be concerned with the two most commonly used clefs, the TREBLE or G clef, and the BASS or F clef. Notice the positions of the clef signs on the staff.

THE LINES AND SPACES

The lines and spaces of the stafs have names that apply to any note that may be on them. Not counting sharps and flats, there are only seven note names: A, B, C, D, E, F and G.

\# b \# b \# b \# b \# b \# b

TREBLE CLEF

LINES   SPACES

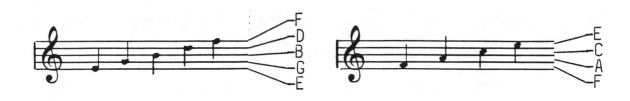

Here is a good way to remember the lines and spaces of the treble clef:
(Always read from the bottom up.)

LINES   E G B D F "Every Good Boy Does Fine."

SPACES F A C E Think of the word "FACE".

BASS CLEF

LINES   SPACES

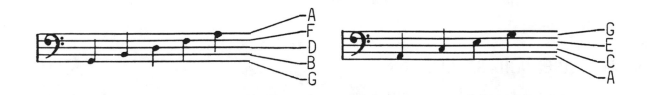

Remembering the lines and spaces of the bass clef:

LINES   G B D F A "Good Boys Do Fine Always."

SPACES A C E G Think of the phrase "ACE (is) Good."

THE GRAND STAFF

Treble and bass stafs together make up the GRAND STAFF. Diagram shows full piano keyboard range with notation for all the white keys.

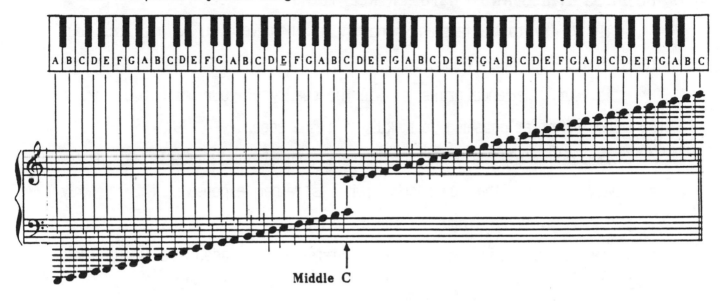

Middle C

KEY SIGNATURES

The key signature is the sharps or flats directly after the clef sign. It indicates in which key the music is to be played. The same key signature can indicate a major key or its relative minor key. Chart shows all keys.

Section 6. Doing Business

BUSINESS ETHICS AND CUSTOMER RELATIONS

Always try to be fair and honest with whomever you do business. Your reputation is your most valuable asset.

As your experience grows, so will the quality of your work, but make a conscious effort at polishing your skills to a fine edge.

Subscribing to The Piano Technician's Journal would greatly aid in this endeavor; however, the subscription price is rather expensive. This monthly magazine is available from The Piano Technician's Guild, an organization of piano technicians throughout the United States and Canada. (See Useful Lists section).

As your standards rise, so will your income. The word gets around. Repeat customers are the life blood of a professional person, and a satisfied customer can be easily approached for a future appointment and also be one of your best means of advertising.

Since the piano technician usually works in the customer's home, he should dress and conduct himself in a professional manner at all times. It makes a favorable impression and is just good business.

ADVERTISING

Satisfied customers are your best advertising but you will also need to use other media. Advertising in the daily newspaper is not too productive for piano service. The weekly Shopper's Guide and similar consumer-oriented small publications will bring better results.

Have some business cards printed and put some on bulletin boards in churches. grocery stores and laundromats. After you are established, you will want to list your services in the telephone directory Yellow Pages.

THE TELEPHONE

The telephone is invaluable in nearly every business operation. If you are away a good part of the time and there is no one there to take your calls, it may pay you to purchase a telephone answering machine.

Have some service forms printed with your company name, etc. so customer information can be recorded in an orderly manner. A copy of this form can also serve as a receipt when you are paid.

When customers call, ask them a few questions so you will know what to expect and what parts to take to the job . Inquire about the type, age and brand name of the piano and ask if it needs repair and when it was tuned last. These inquiries not only give you some information about the piano but also some idea of what sort of person you are dealing with. If the caller sounds too weird, you may decide to tell them your schedule is filled. The telephone is also indispensable in conjunction with your appointment book.

KEEPING AN APPOINTMENT BOOK

When you have reached the point where you have confidence in your work, begin keeping a customer appointment book. Upon finishing a tuning job, politely remind them that their piano should be tuned every six months – but at the very least, once a year. Ask if you may put them in your book and call them for another appointment when the specified time comes around. Most customers are happy to comply with this request as it relieves them of having to remember piano tuning time.

CUSTOMER FILES

Always keep a copy of your service form. When properly filled out, this slip should contain the following information:

Customer's name, address and phone number.

The date of service.

The name, type and serial number of the piano.

Description of the work done.

Price charged for the work.

General condition of the piano.

At the bottom, put the name of something that will remind you of the customer.

Also on the bottom, note when the customer wants to be contacted again: (six months – one year, etc).

On the back of this form, write the directions for getting to the customer's house. Once you have this, you won't have to annoy them by asking directions again.

Keep these slips in order by date, so they may oe easily referred to from your file cards (below).

Acquire a metal file box (these can be had in various lengths to accomodate small or large files) and a quantity of 3 X 5 inch file cards. On the face of these cards put the name, address, phone number, etc. of the customer. On the back, using only one line for each entry, keep a record of the work done, the price and the date. This can be in a condensed code, such as: Ta for tuning to A-440, R for repair, Rg for regulation, etc. Keep these cards in the file box in alphabetical order and update the information on them every month. A good customer file is one of your most valuable possessions.

KEEPING RECORDS

Get an 8-column ledger book from an office supply store. Mark the columns for: Date, Description, Gross Amount, Received or Billed, Tools, Parts, Other Expenses and Net Amount.

Every time you do a job, buy parts or tools, etc. keep your receipt and enter it in this ledger. It will tell you at a glance how your business is doing and greatly simplify taxes and deductions.

BUSINESS LICENSE

If you decide to start your own full-time piano service business, make some inquiries concerning any local and state business licenses that may be required. These usually involve only a small fee, and many states and areas do not charge for an annual renewal unless the company's earnings are over a prescribed amount.

WORKING FOR A PIANO DEALER

Going to work for a piano dealer is an excellent way of getting started and gain valuable experience as a piano technician.

Dealers make all sorts of working arrangements with technicians; part time, full time, in the shop, salary, percentage, salary and percentage. Some dealers give the incoming service calls to a technician in return for his tuning the floor pianos, etc.

Many of the major piano manufacturers insist the dealer have a staff technician before he can aquire the franchise for their line of pianos.

Usually, when a technician decides to leave the employment of a dealer, he takes the following of his steady customers with him.

CLOSING COMMENTS

The scope of information provided in this book ranges from telling a person how to fix a sticking key on their own piano to setting up shop and becoming a piano service technician. Of course, how this information is applied is up to the individual. Remember, nothing enhances knowledge like experience and the sooner you begin to get some, the sooner you will reach your goal. So get going, and best wishes.

Jack Bradley

ABOUT THE AUTHOR

Jack Bradley has been a full-time piano technician for over fifteen years and is a graduate of two piano technician schools. Aside from having his own piano service business, he has headed the piano service department of several large music stores and has, for several years, been the area technician for one of the world's largest piano manufacturers.

He is also a professional pianist and has traveled extensively with bands and groups and worked with many top names in the entertainment world.

Jack Bradley is also the author of "How To Read & Write Music, Including Professional Chord Symbol Method", a book highly acclaimed by many players and teachers.

....

Section 7. Useful Lists

PIANO SUPPLY COMPANIES

American Piano Supply Company
242 South Parkway
P.O.Box 1055
Clifton, NJ 07014
201/777 3600

D.M. Best & Company Ltd.
221 Richmond St. West
Toronto, Ontario M5V 1W2
Canada
416/977 1028

Pacific Piano supply Company
P.O.Box 9412
North Hollywood, CA 91608
213/877 0674

Piano Technicians Supply Company
72 Old Orchard Grove
Toronto, Ontario M5M 2C9
Canada
416/483 9822

Schaff Piano Supply Company
451 Oakwood Road
Lake Zurich, IL 60047
312/438 4556

Tuner's Supply Company
88-94 Wheatland Street
Somerville, MA 02145
617/666 4550

TOOLS

Jensen Tools Inc.
785 So. 46th Street
Phoenix, AZ 85040
602/968 6231

U.S. General Supply Company
100 Commercial Street
Plainview, NY 11803
800/605 7077

ORGANIZATIONS

Piano Technicians Guild, Inc.
940 Ward Parkway
Kansas City, MO 64114
816/444 3500

National Piano Manufacturers
Association Of America.
15080 Bethwood Parkway,
Suite 108
Dallas, TX 75381
214/241 8457

PIANO MANUFACTURERS

Aeolian Corporation
2722 Pershing Avenue
Memphis, TN 38112
901/542 1151

Baldwin Piano & Organ Company
1801 Gilbert Avenue
Cincinatti, OH 45202
513/652 7806

Everett Piano Company
900 Indiana Avenue
South Haven, MI 49090
616/637 2194

Kawai American Corporation
24220 So. Vermont Aveune
Harbor City, CA 90710
213/534 2350

Kohler & Campbell, Inc.
P.O.Box 448
Granite Falls, NC 28630
704/396 3376

Kimball International, Inc.
P.O.Box 460
Jasper, IN 47546
812/482 1600

Marantz Piano Company
P.O.Box 460
Morganton, NC 28655
704/437 7135

Samick Music Corporation
14235 Lomitas Avenue
La Puente, CA 91746
213/968 5550

Sohmer & Company, Inc.
11-02-16 31st Avenue
Long Island City, NY 11106
212/274 8300

Steinway & Sons
Steinway Place
Long Island City, NY 11105
212/721 2600

Story & Clark Piano Company
100 Fulton Avenue
Grand Haven, MI 49417
616/842 6000

The Wurlitzer Company
403 East Gurler Road
DeKalb, IL 60115
815/756 2771

Yamaha International Corporation
6600 Orangethorpe Avenue
Buena Park, CA 90620
714/522 9451

Young Chang America, Inc.
417 East Platt Street
Tampa. FL 33602
813/229 7171

SOME SAMPLE CHARGES

Tuning: not more than 2 times over and raising pitch no more than 1/4 tone.
$40.00

Raising pitch over 1/4 tone - for each additional tuning over original 2 times over.
$15.00

Complete regulation of vertical action (in piano) including new underfelts, setting dip, etc.
$100.00

Complete regulation of grand action (in shop) including new underfelts, etc.
$150.00

Install complete set white key tops (includes leveling keys and capstan regulation).
$135.00

Install complete set keytops; whites and sharps (includes leveling keys and capstan regulation.
$175.00

Repair work: per hour.
$35.00

Glossary

Action: The mechanism in the piano that transmits key movement to the hammers striking the strings.

After-Touch: The very slight drop of a piano key when the jack releases the hammer.

Agraffe: Brass string guides screwed into the plate near the tuning pins.

Backcheck: A sort of brake for the hammer movement.

Back Stop: An extension of the hammer butt that is caught by the backcheck.

Billings Flange: A metal flange that encircles the center pin.

Capstan: A screw near the back end of a key, for regulating out slack (lost motion).

Damper: A felt-faced block which stops the vibration of a string(s).

Dip: The travel distance of a key from at rest till it hits bottom.

Drop Action: The action of a spinet, constructed to function below the level of the keys and connected to them by sticker wires and elbows.

Drop Screw: A small screw tapped through the hammer shank of the grand that limits the upward movement of the repetition lever.

Elbow: The curved joint at the bottom end of the sticker wire of a spinet to connect the key to the action. Elbows are made of wood or plastic.

False Beat: A pulsating sound produced by a single string; usually caused by a flaw or bend in the string.

Flange: A wooden (sometimes metal) hinge-like device that attaches the moving parts to the action rails.

Flats: The black keys; same as sharps except flats _lower_ the pitch of a tone one half step.

Hammer: The felt mallet that strikes the piano strings.

Hysteresis: In pianos, the tedency of a string to seek the tension it has been in the longest time.

Inharmonicity: The sound quality caused by the stiffness of piano strings that causes the tuner to raise or "stretch" the frequencies in the upper treble.

Interval: The distance between two tones.

Jack: The wooden part of the action that pushes the hammer butt toward the string. Sometimes called the "fly".

Key Button: A felt-lined soft wood guide, located in the middle of the key for the purpose of guiding the key up and down and right and left.

Key Dip Block: A small block of wood used for measuring the depth of a depressed key; either 3/8" or 7/16".

Knuckle: The small, barrel-like cushion on the underside of the grand hammer shank. It takes the push of the jack.

Let-Off: The release of the jack.

Node: A zero point in the vibration of a string.

Partial: A natural subdivision of a vibrating string or air column.

Pin Block: The laminated wood plank into which the tuning pins are driven.

Pitch: The level of frequency, or highness or lowness of a sound.

Repetition Lever: That part of the grand action that facilitates speed by allowing the hammer to be played again as soon as it is released from check.

Sharps: The black keys; used to raise the pitch of a tone one half step. (Also used as flats.)

Soundboard: The wooden diaphragm of a piano that supports the bridges and magnifies the sound.

Soundboard Crown: The convex configuration of a soundboard.

Soundboard Shim: A wedge-shaped strip of wood, glued into soundboard cracks.

Sticker: The connecting piece between the capstan and the wippen. Also called "abstract". There are no stickers in the console or grand pianos.

Tuning Hammer: Tuning lever.

Wippen: A lever in the piano action for conveying motion from the key to the hammer.

Index